Moodle 2 for Teaching 7-14 Year Olds

Beginner's Guide

Effective e-learning for younger students, using Moodle as your classroom assistant

Mary Cooch

BIRMINGHAM - MUMBAI

Moodle 2 for Teaching 7-14 Year Olds
Beginner's Guide

First edition: March 2009

Second edition: May 2012

Production Reference: 1090512

Published by Packt Publishing Ltd.
Livery Place
35 Livery Street
Birmingham B3 2PB, UK.

ISBN 978-1-84951-832-1

www.packtpub.com

Cover Image by Asher Wishkerman (a.wishkerman@mpic.de)

Credits

Author

Mary Cooch

Reviewers

Dr. Nellie Deutsch

Louise Adele Jakobsen

Ben Reynolds

Acquisition Editors

David Barnes

Sarah Cullington

Lead Technical Editor

Arun Nadar

Technical Editor

Naheed Shaikh

Project Coordinators

Kushal Bhardwaj

Alka Nayak

Proofreader

Mario Cecere

Indexer

Hemangini Bari

Production Coordinator

Melwyn D'sa

Cover Work

Melwyn D'sa

About the Author

Mary Cooch, or Moodlefairy, as she is known online, has taught Languages and Geography at Our Lady's High School, Preston, UK for over 25 years. She now spends part of her working week travelling Europe showing teachers, lecturers, or business users how best to use Moodle, and the other part liaising with the ten primary schools linked to her own high school. Based on her personal experiences, Mary has a deep understanding of what works best with younger students, and empathy (being a non-technical user herself) with teachers who just want to use Moodle as a teaching tool without understanding all the geeky stuff behind it. Mary lives, eats, sleeps, and breathes Moodle and you will find her helping out on the forums of www.moodle.org or via the training centre based at her school www.ourlearning.co.uk. Mary will go anywhere to help you Moodle!

Mary is also the author of *Moodle 2 First Look*, the first ever book about the new features of Moodle 2. She also helps write the documentation on the main Moodle site, www.moodle.org and blogs on www.moodleblog.net.

I would like to thank Steve for his support, Estelle for her eloquence, and Chris for his commitment. I would like to acknowledge my Moodle Manager Assistant Head at Our Lady's Mark Greenwood for his muse, Moodle Community Manager Helen Foster for her help, and last but not least Founder and Lead Developer Martin Dougiamas for his Moodle.

About the Reviewers

Dr. Nellie Deutsch has been teaching English to speakers of other languages since the mid 70s. She has been integrating technology into her classes since the mid 90s. Nellie earned her doctorate in education and educational leadership with a specialization in curriculum and instruction from the University of Phoenix from the School of Advanced Studies in 2010. Her dissertation research (available on ProQuest, Amazon) focused on instructor experiences with integrating technology in blended learning contexts in higher education around the world.

Nellie is the founder of Integrating Technology for Active Lifelong Learning (IT4ALL), an online informal network of volunteers that provides free professional development workshops for groups around the world, generally in conjunction with different projects and initiatives. Dr. Deutsch is also the founder and current coordinator of the annual Connecting Online for Instruction and Learning and Moodlemoot free online conferences, hosted online by Integrating Technology and supported by WiZiQ online learning platform. Dr. Deutsch has provided consultation on how to integrate Moodle and Elluminate learning environments for distance education at Open University of Israel, and worked as a consultant for WikiEducator. org, supported by the Commonwealth of Learning (COL), Otago Polytechnic (New Zealand), and Athabasca Open University (Canada) in developing online courses and facilitation.

Nellie mentors educators to use technology to enhance student learning using Moodle, WebQuests, Professional Electronic Portfolios (Mahara), Web 2.0 tools, social networks, and wikis. In addition, she is an accredited PAIRS (Practical Application of Intimate Relationship Skills), conflict resolution, and Reiki practitioner. She practices Mindfulness Meditation and the Alexander Technique.

Dr. Deutsch has written chapters in books on the use of technology and research (Cases in Online Interviews) and has peer-reviewed articles and books on technology-enhanced learning. Dr. Deutsch also serves as chair for doctoral students. She is currently researching and writing a book on learning with Moodle.

Finally, Dr. Deutsch has presented on integrating technology into the classroom and educational leadership at conferences in the United States and virtually around the world. Nellie organized and chaired a panel discussion on the merits and challenges of integrating technology into the classroom at the International Leadership Association (ILA) in London, in 2011. She will also present and facilitate Moodle for Teachers workshop at the TESOL, Philadelphia conference on culture in the English classroom in 2012.

Louise Adele Jakobsen is passionate about the potential a wide range of technologies have to enhance learning and support teaching, business, and life. Recent roles and responsibilities which have enhanced her knowledge, understanding, and application of a variety of tools include being the eLearning Curriculum Manager at a large Further Education (FE) College in the UK with responsibility for moving forward the eLearning agenda; supporting and encouraging staff to use Moodle in more interactive and engaging ways, and Learning and Development Manager at a private training organization where Moodle was used to support organisational and work-based development. Her enthusiasm is evident through the various training, sharing, and motivating strategies that are used. She has experience of working in FE, Higher Education, Adult and Community Learning, and Local Government delivering high class training to teachers, managers, care staff, and small and medium businesses. Louise has also developed resources and delivered training for and on behalf of national organisations including NIACE and THinK FE. She completed her MSc in Multimedia and eLearning with the University of Huddersfield (UK) in 2008. Her interests/ experiences include teaching and learning, technology, eLearning pedagogies, effective use of VLEs (especially Moodle), designing and reviewing eLearning resources, using social networking tools in education, staff development/training and change management.

Louise authored the chapter *Embedding eLearning in Further Education* which was published in the book Applied eLearning and eTeaching in HE in 2008 and reviewed the Packt Publishing book Moodle 2.0 Multimedia Cookbook in 2011.

> I would like to thank my husband and daughter for their support through all my academic, professional, and personal pursuits and challenges.

Ben Reynolds is a Senior Program Manager of CTYOnline at The Johns Hopkins University's Center for Talented Youth (CTY). An award-winning fictionist, he began CTY's face-to-face writing program in 1978 and launched CTYOnline's writing program in 1983. He began administrating CTYOnline's writing and language arts division in 1985. CTYOnline serves over 10,000 students a year in writing/language arts, math, science, computer science, Advanced Placement, and foreign languages. In the 1990's, Reynolds left the classroom for full-time administration both of CTY's writing/language arts program and of a residential site for CTY Summer Programs. Reynolds has also taught writing and the teaching of writing for the Johns Hopkins School of Continuing Studies. He holds a BA from Duke University, where he part-timed in the computer center, trading print out for punch cards, and an MA from Johns Hopkins in Fiction Writing. He is an active member of the Using Moodle community and has reviewed several Packt publications.

www.PacktPub.com

Support files, eBooks, discount offers and more

You might want to visit www.PacktPub.com for support files and downloads related to your book.

Did you know that Packt offers eBook versions of every book published, with PDF and ePub files available? You can upgrade to the eBook version at www.PacktPub.com and as a print book customer, you are entitled to a discount on the eBook copy. Get in touch with us at service@packtpub.com for more details.

At www.PacktPub.com, you can also read a collection of free technical articles, sign up for a range of free newsletters and receive exclusive discounts and offers on Packt books and eBooks.

http://PacktLib.PacktPub.com

Do you need instant solutions to your IT questions? PacktLib is Packt's online digital book library. Here, you can access, read and search across Packt's entire library of books.

Why Subscribe?

- ◆ Fully searchable a`cross every book published by Packt
- ◆ Copy and paste, print and bookmark content
- ◆ On demand and accessible via web browser

Free Access for Packt account holders

If you have an account with Packt at www.PacktPub.com, you can use this to access PacktLib today and view nine entirely free books. Simply use your login credentials for immediate access.

Table of Contents

Preface

Moodle 2 For Teaching 7-14 Year Olds is not a book for geeks. This book will not tell you about PHP, HTML, or anything else that you don't need to know. This is a practical book for teachers, written by a teacher with two decades of practical experience, latterly in using Moodle to motivate younger students. The aim of this book is to give you some hints and advice on how to get your Moodle course up and running with useful content that your students will actually want to go and learn from on a regular basis.

We will assume that you have an installation of Moodle that is managed by somebody else so that you are only responsible for creating and delivering course content. Throughout the book, we will be building a course from scratch, adaptable for ages 7-14, on Rivers and Flooding. It could be any topic however, as Moodle lends itself to all subjects and people of all ages.

What this book covers

Chapter 1, *Getting Started*, teaches us how to capture the attention of our young students and entice them into our course. It starts with a blank course page and looks at how to brighten this up with useful side blocks, colorful fonts, and attractive images.

Chapter 2, *Adding Worksheets and Resources*, teaches how to upload to our course page lessons, homeworks, and worksheets that we have already made in programs such as Microsoft Word or PowerPoint. We will also learn how to use Moodle's own pages to create lessons directly online.

Chapter 3, *Getting Interactive*, gets the students to interact with us, the teachers, and with each other in Moodle. The chapter combines classroom tasks with Moodle activities in a role play project which will get the students thinking and collaborating. We'll also find out how to get them to send work to us through Moodle which we can mark online with Moodle's gradebook recording their scores for us.

Chapter 4, *Self-marking Quizzes*, gives us ideas for introducing, practicing, and consolidating learning through the use of online activities such as quizzes, matching exercises, and crosswords. We learn how, at the click of a button, we can have differentiated exercises for students of varying abilities – and then go have a break while Moodle does all the marking!

Chapter 5, *Games*, teaches us how to enhance learning with some easy-to-set-up games, one of which Moodle can mark for us. So while the students are enjoying playing, the gradebook is keeping the scores updated.

Chapter 6, *Multimedia*, is concerned with sound and vision. Here we get the students involved in producing multimedia content for Moodle—and get creative ourselves too!

Chapter 7, *Wonderful Web 2.0*, harnesses what the children are already familiar with by looking at some free online applications that can be used in Moodle by both us and our young students.

Chapter 8, *Practicalities*, deals with the "nitty gritty" of uploading and displaying resources in Moodle. It explains how to ensure everything works properly, not just for teachers but also for students. We learn how to make resources accessible to children who don't have Microsoft Office. We discover alternative methods of displaying worksheets and slideshows, investigate ways of resizing images for our course page, and learn about the pros and cons of using Moodle on tablets and mobiles.

Chapter 9, *Advanced tips and tricks*, gives us a taste of Moodle Level 2! It looks at how we can use the more advanced features of Moodle, plus some optional extras, to enhance our teaching further. We learn how to create decision-making exercises and surveys, how to set up our course so that students can only move on after they have met our criteria and how they can view their progress as they go along. We end our journey by making our course page look more like a web page.

What you need for this book

No specific technologies are needed, although it is assumed that the reader will play the role of a teacher in a Moodle course that is set up for them. It is desirable, though not essential, to have access to Microsoft Word and Powerpoint.

Who this book is for

This book is for regular, non-technical teachers of pre-teen or early teenage children. It assumes no prior knowledge of Moodle and no particular expertise on the web. Classroom assistants may also find this book a very useful resource.

Conventions

In this book, you will find several headings appearing frequently.

To give clear instructions of how to complete a procedure or task, we use:

Time for action – heading

1. Action 1
2. Action 2
3. Action 3

Instructions often need some extra explanation so that they make sense, so they are followed with:

What just happened?

This heading explains the working of tasks or instructions that you have just completed.

You will also find some other learning aids in the book, including:

Have a go hero – heading

These set practical challenges and give you ideas for experimenting with what you have learned.

You will also find a number of styles of text that distinguish between different kinds of information. Here are some examples of these styles, and an explanation of their meaning.

Code words in text are shown as follows: "It should end in either `.jpg` or `.png` or `.gif`."

New terms and **important words** are shown in bold. Words that you see on the screen, in menus or dialog boxes for example, appear in the text like this: "In **Course summary**, write a sentence or two to explain what the course is about."

 Warnings or important notes appear in a box like this.

 Tips and tricks appear like this.

Reader feedback

Feedback from our readers is always welcome. Let us know what you think about this book—what you liked or may have disliked. Reader feedback is important for us to develop titles that you really get the most out of.

To send us general feedback, simply send an e-mail to `feedback@packtpub.com`, and mention the book title through the subject of your message.

If there is a topic that you have expertise in and you are interested in either writing or contributing to a book, see our author guide on `www.packtpub.com/authors`.

Customer support

Now that you are the proud owner of a Packt book, we have a number of things to help you to get the most from your purchase.

Errata

Although we have taken every care to ensure the accuracy of our content, mistakes do happen. If you find a mistake in one of our books—maybe a mistake in the text or the code—we would be grateful if you would report this to us. By doing so, you can save other readers from frustration and help us improve subsequent versions of this book. If you find any errata, please report them by visiting `http://www.packtpub.com/support`, selecting your book, clicking on the **errata submission form** link, and entering the details of your errata. Once your errata are verified, your submission will be accepted and the errata will be uploaded to our website, or added to any list of existing errata, under the Errata section of that title.

Piracy

Piracy of copyright material on the Internet is an ongoing problem across all media. At Packt, we take the protection of our copyright and licenses very seriously. If you come across any illegal copies of our works, in any form, on the Internet, please provide us with the location address or website name immediately so that we can pursue a remedy.

Please contact us at `copyright@packtpub.com` with a link to the suspected pirated material.

We appreciate your help in protecting our authors, and our ability to bring you valuable content.

Questions

You can contact us at questions@packtpub.com if you are having a problem with any aspect of the book, and we will do our best to address it.

1
Getting Started

We're at the very start of our journey here. We know where we are heading—we want to create a fun-filled, interesting, interactive, and informative learning environment for our young students. We want them to have access to all of our resources that would normally be on paper, plus any new activities that we hope are out there, but that we haven't actually discovered! Ideally, we'd like a situation where our initial efforts will be rewarded by saving us a lot of time in the long term. We want Moodle to occupy our students usefully, mark their work, and record their scores so that we don't have to do it. A tall order, but one that is perfectly possible!

In this chapter, we shall:

- Take a tour of the Moodle course page to get familiar with all of the options that we have; so that we are ready to set it up for our classes
- Choose the most suitable layout for our course, and make each section attractive to the students
- Take a look, add, and edit the blocks on either side of our work area to make these blocks useful for us and our class
- Add text and images to our work area to improve its appearance
- Learn how to make *click here* links to various websites for our students to easily access them

First impressions

Let's assume you've been given an empty Moodle course page. When you first go to your course page, you'll probably see something that looks like this:

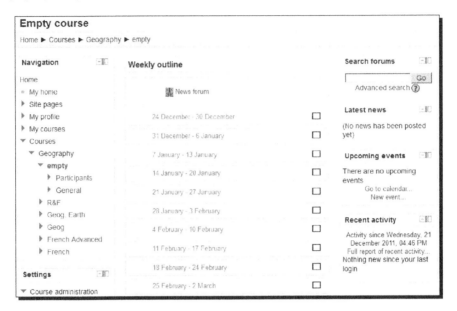

Don't be disheartened if this doesn't mean much to you at this stage. If you were to flick through to the end of the book, you would find our completed work far more welcoming:

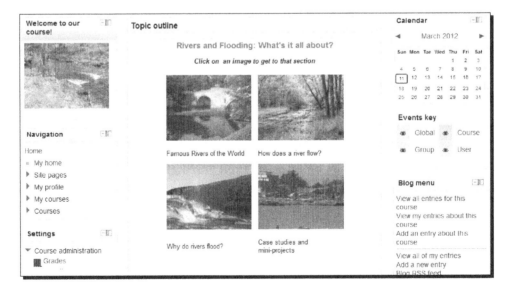

Let's go back to that first screenshot, of the **empty** course.

 Don't be put off by the word *course*. A course can be anything you want it to be—a teacher's class page, a single unit of work (such as ours), a project, a year's lessons shared among a group of teachers, and so on.

There are three columns; two narrow ones on the right and left, containing some blocks, and a wider column in the middle. This wider column is the work area, to which we will start adding our teaching materials (this will be covered in detail in *Chapter 2*, *Adding Worksheets and Resources*).

The name of the course (**empty**, for now) appears on the upper left, and an abbreviated version (**empty**) will appear in the bar below it (the bar is called a **navigation bar**). The block called **Navigation** shows different things to students and teachers, but basically it helps us find our way around the Moodle site.

The **Settings** block has a **Course administration** area just for the teachers. It allows us (teachers) to perform various actions for our course. Let's start by changing the course name to what we want, and setting up the work area to something more suitable for us.

Time for action – customizing our course page

We're going to change the course name and add some sections in the central area for our work!

1. In the **Settings** block, click the arrow next to **Course administration** and then click on **Edit settings**.

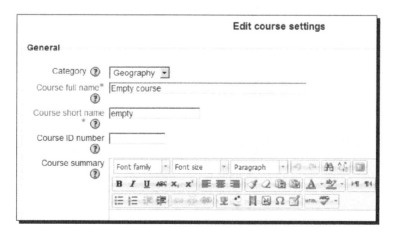

2. Next to **Course full name**, type in the full name of your course (such as **Rivers and Flooding**).

3. Next to **Course short name**, give your course an abbreviation, which will be seen on the navigation bar. For our example course, we'll use **R & F**.

4. In **Course summary**, write a sentence or two to explain what the course is about.

5. Scroll down to the sections shown in the following screenshot:

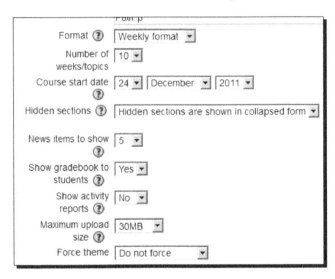

6. For **Format**, you can use **Weekly format** to include one section per week, or select **Topic format** to use numbered sections that you can set up as you like. For this example, we will select **Topic format**. (You might have other options, but these are the two most useful ones for us).

7. In the **Number of weeks/topics** field, choose the number of days, weeks, or topics that you want to include on your course page (you can change this at any time). For this example, we will specify **4**.

8. If you want your course to start on a particular date (and not immediately), specify this date in the **Course start date** field.

   For now, as a beginner, this much will be enough.

 If at first you don't know what it means, it's safe to ignore it! This applies to Moodle activities as well as the course settings.

9. Click on **Save changes**. Your course page should now look something like this:

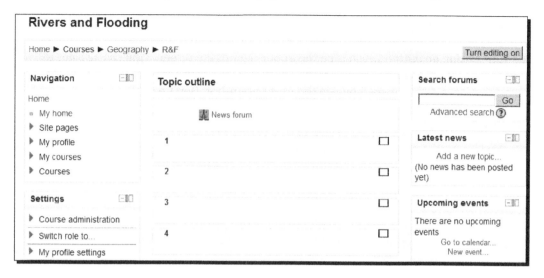

What just happened?

We just began customizing our course page the way we want it to look. We've now got the title we want, and the middle section (where our work will go) is now divided into separate numbered sections—four, for us—which will help us to organize our project.

At the moment, there's nothing next to these numbers. We need to get into each section, give it a heading, and prepare it so that we can add our worksheets and lessons, which we will do in future chapters of this book. There's something called **News forum** too, which I'll describe later.

We've also still got those blocks on either side. We need the **Navigation** block to find our way around, and the **Settings** block lets us organize our course and lets everyone manage their profiles—but what about the others? What are they for? Do we need them? How do we change them? In fact, how do we change anything on the page?

Making changes on the course page

If you point your cursor at one of the sections in the middle and start typing—nothing happens! We can't actually add any text or make any alterations until we have clicked on the **Turn editing on** button which is on the upper-right of the screen. (You can also get to it by clicking into the **Course administration** section of the **Settings** block). When you do, everything looks different, as shown in the next screenshot. Don't panic!

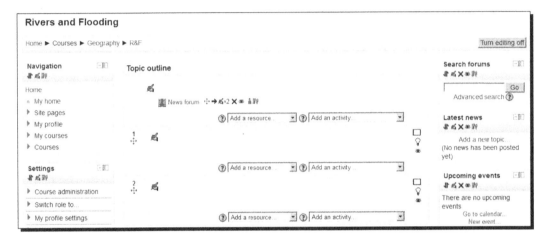

A lot of symbols (icons) have appeared. These icons have different roles in helping us to edit the course. They help us to add content, delete content, duplicate content, or alter what's already there. Let's take a tour of the blocks, and use this as a way to understand these icons.

Getting the best out of the side blocks

Every course in Moodle has a central work area and a selection of blocks on either side. These blocks serve various purposes such as telling you the latest news, letting you know who's online, displaying quiz results, and so on.

Shortly, we'll have a look at the blocks available, and I'll give you my thoughts on how useful they might be. Some schools may decide for you which blocks you must have, and the blocks that should be made *sticky* throughout Moodle and some schools might have decided only to have blocks on one side. If you're allowed to have your own blocks on both sides, then the next section will show you how you can move them around and take away the ones that you don't really need.

First, let's take a closer look at the **Activities** block. The following screenshot shows the **Activities** block, although the icons shown are available in every block. According to your Moodle course's theme (its appearance or "skin") these icons might be a little different from those pictured here:

Time for action – moving, adding, and deleting blocks

We're going to look at how we can deal with the side blocks!

1. To hide a block from students, click on the eye. (You will still be able to see it grayed out). Click again to make it visible to students.

2. To choose where else to display this block, click on the hand/pen icon. If you're unsure, leave it.

3. To delete a block from the course page, click on **X**. (You can add it again later; it's not gone forever).

4. To move a block, click on the arrows and then click inside a box with dotted lines that is where you want to move it to. (Boxes will appear once you click the arrow).

5. To add a new block, find the block called **Add a block**, and then click on **Add** (as shown in the following screenshot):

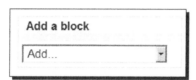

6. The face icons are used to set who can see and edit the blocks (ignore these for now).

7. To keep a block out of the way while you're working on a course page (known as "docking" it) click into the slim, central box (numbered as **1**) as shown in the following screenshot. It will then bounce to the left of your screen, with its name vertically displayed. To get it back, click its name and then click the right box (numbered as **2**) as shown in the following screenshot:

What just happened?

We've learned how to deal with the blocks that appear on either sides of our central work area. Let's now take a look at what they all do.

Useful and less useful blocks

Here's a table of the standard blocks that are available in Moodle, and that you could have on your course page (if you're allowed). I've explained what they do, and what I think about them:

Block name	What it does	Why use it
Activities	Shows the different activities that you've set up.	If you want your students to get to certain activities quickly, or see them listed.
Navigation	How you get to different parts of Moodle.	This block follows everyone everywhere in Moodle!
Settings	Where you can organize your course and everyone can manage their profile.	This block appears on course pages and each activity has its own **Settings** block too.
Blog menu/tags	Allows you to add and view blog entries and keywords in blogs.	Not really necessary as a block (we look at blogs in *Chapter 6, Multimedia*).
Calendar	A calendar is where you can show course, individual, or site wide events.	Useful if you have a lot of events that you want to remind your students about.
Comments	Allows people to add comments.	Useful block to add in lots of places for feedback.
Community finder	If an admin has turned this on, you can search other Moodles for useful resources.	Worth a look if it is turned on for you.
Course completion status	Lets you see the progress of students towards finishing the course.	We'll look at this advanced block in the final chapter.
Courses	Lists students courses.	A quick way for them to get around their courses.
Course description	Shows the course summary that you put in the course settings.	Not really essential—they're doing the course now, after all!
Feedback	A way in which an admin gets feedback from students on all courses.	Later we'll look at how you can get your own feedback.

Block name	What it does	Why use it
HTML	A blank block for your own use.	Very handy—more details later.
Latest news	Displays what's in the news forum.	If you want that, it's fine!
Logged in user	Shows a picture and details of the logged in user.	Could be a nice touch but not essential.
Mentees block	Advanced block allowing mentors to "watch" students.	We don't need it at this stage.
Messages	Moodle's instant messaging service.	Needs to be switched on by your admin; useful for instant communication, but younger students may find it very distracting!
My private files	A way for everyone to store their own stuff.	Handy block for your students—good one to add.
Online users	Shows who's accessing your course online at the moment.	Useful for making sure that everyone's there, on task.
People	Lists those enrolled in your course, and when they last visited your course page.	Another useful block to keep a check on your participants.
Quiz results	Displays recent quiz results.	Handy for encouraging competition among students, by providing a league table of scores.
Recent activity	Who's done what and when.	Useful for students to see what's new, and for teachers to see who's sent in their work.
Recent blog entries	A quick link to blogs about your course.	Useful if you are using blogs in your course.
Random glossary entry	Shows a glossary entry at a certain time (if you've got a glossary).	Think about this when we are making a glossary in *Chapter 3*, *Getting Interactive*; it's up to you.
Remote RSS feeds	Shows news feeds of your choice.	Can be very useful—we'll look at this in the final chapter.
Search forums	Allows students to search through forum entries.	Don't bother with this; I've never found it useful for my classes.
Section links	A quick way to get to a numbered section.	If you want to, fine, but you can click the links in the **Navigation** bar instead.

Block name	What it does	Why use it
Self completion	A way in which students can mark their course as finished.	We'll look at this advanced block in the final chapter
Tags	Makes a "cloud" of tags which people have added.	Pretty—but can be dangerous if your students added unsuitable tags!
Upcoming events	Information about what's coming soon, taken from the calendar or activity deadlines.	If you have a lot of events or deadlines it's useful.

Have a go hero – get the right choice of blocks for your course!

Ok, now it's time to put the theory into practice! For our purposes, the best blocks will probably be the ones listed as follows. Using the instructions on the previous pages, delete the ones we don't want, add the new ones, and then arrange them equally on either side of the middle section! Let's have:

- A **People** block
- A **My private files** block
- A **Comments** block
- A **Calendar** block
- A **Messages** block
- An **HTML** block (which we'll customize now)

Making our own side blocks in Moodle

Let's take a closer look at the HTML block that you just added:

Time for action – configuring an HTML block

Let's learn how to configure an HTML block for our course page.

1. Click on the editing icon in your HTML block.

2. In the **Block title** field, enter something for use as the title of your block.

3. In the **Content** field, type a few words of welcome:

4. Click on **Save changes**.

What just happened?

We made a side block of our own! At the moment, it only has a couple of words in it (and a smiley in my case, although you'll only have one if your admin has enabled them). Later in this chapter, you'll add an image and we'll make it the 'Welcome' block for our new course. I like to use HTML blocks with images to brighten up the page—younger students appreciate this. You can even set them up so that you can click on the image to get to a particular website, which is both attractive and useful.

As we did this, we came across the editing box—which we'll call the text editor—for the first time, into which we can type text and add images. (It's sometimes called the **TinyMCE** editor or HTML editor too and is like some text editors you might see on blogs or online forums). We're going to investigate it further now as we venture into the middle section—the main focus of our students' learning.

HTML is just a term meaning website code. An **HTML block** is one where we can add text that Moodle interprets as code, and displays as we wish. Likewise, in the text editor, we can type the words as we want them to appear, and Moodle will code them (with HTML) to make that happen.

We don't need to understand HTML in order to get Moodle to work for us.

Customizing the middle section

It is finally time to get to grips with the middle section—the one we shall be focusing on in the next few chapters. So far, our **Rivers and Flooding** course has got four empty topic sections. Our next task is to get them ready for action—ready for the materials that we will create and upload, from the next chapter onwards.

If you look at the following screenshot, you will see that at the top it says **Topic outline**. We cannot change these words easily, but we can use the blank space at the top to provide a short description of what our course is about, and we can add headings to each of the four sections.

Remember that to do anything on this page now, we need to have editing turned on (via the button on the upper right) and then, in order to type directly into Moodle, we have to click on the pen, hand, or paper icon that we had came across in the HTML block. You can see one above the **News forum**, and one next to the numbered sections:

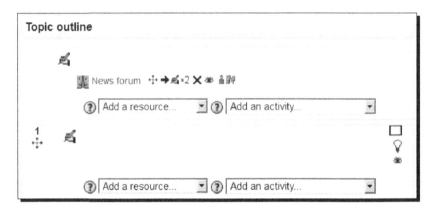

Clicking on the very top one, above the **News forum**, sends us to a page—**Summary of General**. It would be the same if we had clicked on any of the numbered topics (or weeks, if you've chosen them). It would say **Summary of week/topic** and provide a textbox in the text editor.

Using the text editor

We enter our descriptions/headings directly into this box. You will recognize some of the icons from many popular word processing programs, and if you move your cursor over a particular icon, it will give you a hint as to what it does. Younger children like bright colors in a large font, so I'm going to make my headings big and red, but it's worth bearing in mind here that you might have children in your class who are color blind or have other visual impairments, so check with your Special Educational needs specialist which would be the safe colors to use.

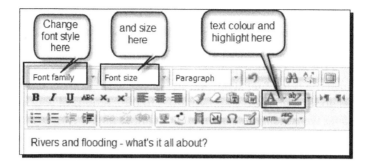

Go along the layers of icons and find out what they do. Type in some text and experiment! Some are pretty self-explanatory. The following table explains a few of the icons you might find useful, but that are less obvious. The numbers in the table refer to the icons in the following screenshot:

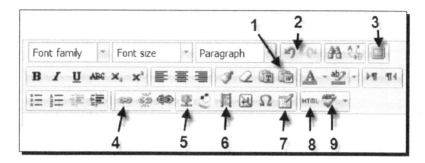

Icon	What it does
1	Improves the look of your text if you paste it directly from Microsoft Word.
2	Lets you cancel what you just did and revert to an earlier stage.
3	Enlarges the text box to make it easier for you to see and type.
4	Lets you create a link to a website or an online file.
5	Lets you insert an image.
6	Allows you to easily add sound or videos.
7	Lets you create a table to improve the layout of your text area.
8	Lets you into the HTML code area (some uses for us later!)
9	Allows you to check the spellings of words you type.

Once you've typed in your text and adapted it according to your requirements, scroll down and click on **Save changes**. Only then will your efforts be visible on the main course page. Until that moment, you can change whatever you wish.

Have a go hero – give titles to each section of your course

We have just given a heading to Topic 0—the top section of our course. If you click on the editing icon for each of the other four topics, you can do exactly the same with them. Remember to change the color, font style, and size (if you wish) from a rather uninteresting default style. Either go for it and add your own titles to the sections of your course, or practice with the ones we're going to use in our ongoing example. They are:

- **Famous Rivers of the World**
- **How does a river flow?**
- **Why do rivers flood?**
- **Flooding case studies**

Want to make your section headings easy to see in the Navigation block?

If you take out the check in *Use default section name* as shown in the following screenshot, and then add your title, the section heading will appear in the **Navigation** block once you've added some resources. If you type into the text editor box instead, it will just show the section number.

Use default section name	☐
Section name	Famous Rivers of the World

What just happened?

We now have headings for each of our topic sections. The page looks more personal and brighter already! A few photographs would enhance it though; let's put some on our course page now!

Brightening up the course page with images

"What is the use of a book", said Alice, "without pictures?"

I'm sometimes fortunate enough to be given temporary access to other schools' Moodle sites. Almost invariably, the websites that are most successful in attracting the young students are the ones that catch the eye immediately on entering the course. Those with nothing more than the default text and a long list of exercises (usually named worksheet 1, worksheet 2, and so on) are barren and lonely places, devoid of any youthful spirit.

I can't emphasize this enough—we as adults might think it's the content that matters (and of course, that's true), but our children will be drawn into our Moodle course by a colorful photo or a smiley icon. Once they're there, we can help them learn!

We don't have to be qualified web designers to make our course page more attractive. We've made a start already, with our headings. Let's now add a small, relevant photo to each topic section. By small, I mean a photo with a size of not more than 200 x 200 pixels (we'll look at photo resizing in *Chapter 7, Wonderful Web 2.0*). Although you can upload a large photo and resize it by dragging at its edges, this distorts the image in Moodle, and doesn't display it as well as it should.

You can't really copy and paste images from Google onto your course page. Apart from copyright issues, this doesn't always work. You might be able to get away with this in PowerPoint, but in Moodle, it's more reliable if you save your chosen image to your hard drive first, and then upload it. We'll take a look at copyright later on.

Time for action – uploading images to our Moodle page

Now that we have set up our Moodle course page, let's make it a little more attractive by adding images.

1. Turn on editing.

2. Click on the editing icon for a topic section (for us, **Topic 1**).

3. Click on the icon that helps you insert an image, as shown in the following screenshot:

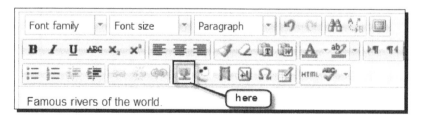

4. In the box that is displayed next, click into **Find or upload an image**:

5. In the box that is displayed next, click on **Upload a file** (**1**) and then click the **Browse** or **Choose file** button (**2**) to locate the image that you want on your computer. (It should end in either `.jpg` or `.png` or `.gif`).

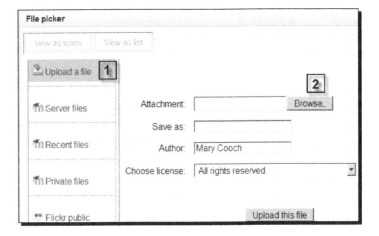

6. Select your image and then click on **Open**, and it will appear in the **Browse** box.

7. You don't need to save it with a different name or select an author or even choose a license. None of these will affect who can see it.

8. Click on the **Upload this file** button.

9. Your image will be previewed in the next screen:

10. In the **Image description** box, add some descriptive text, explaining the photo. Don't just say photo! (The description box for visually-impaired children who will have the words read to them by a machine and they'll know it's a photo already).

11. Click on **Insert**.

12. Click on **Save changes** to make the image appear on your course page.

What just happened?

We've now added our first image to our Moodle course page to brighten it up! It probably seems like an extremely long-winded way of adding an image, but that's only because it's the first time that we did it. I can add images now in a matter of seconds; you will be able to do so as well, with practice. Just bear in mind the following points:

◆ Get your image to the right size before you upload it to Moodle. While there are ways to change its size once you've uploaded it, it isn't the best way forward. Make sure that you are uploading an image file—usually having the extension .jpg, .png, or .gif (more on this, later).

◆ Don't copy and paste an image from the internet. If the site—that the image comes from—ever goes offline, your image will vanish, and you'll end up with a red X.

What if you don't have any good images on your computer?

While it's not advisable (as we said) to copy and paste any random image from Google, you might have noticed, when we clicked the image icon in the text editor to upload our picture, that there was a link in that list on the left to the well-known photo-sharing site, **Flickr**.

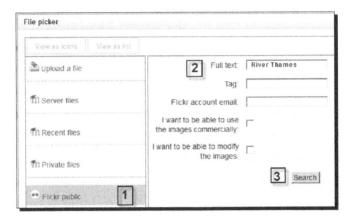

If your admin allows it, then you're able to search sites such as Flickr or Picasa Web albums and use one of their available photos (if you want to add an image).

If I click on the **Flickr public** link (**1**) (instead of **Upload a file**) then I can type in some keywords into the **Full text** field (**2**), or add some tags, or even sign in to my own Flickr account and get a good picture to pretty up my course page.

The next screenshot shows what happened when I typed in **River Thames** and then hit the **Search** button (**3**):

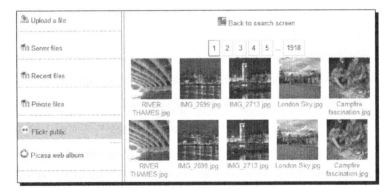

I click on the image that I'd like to use, then on the next screen, click **Select this file**.
If I only want to link to it (and not import it into my course), I check the **Link external** box:

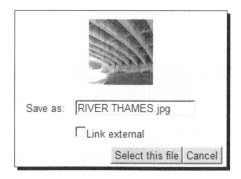

Save as: RIVER THAMES.jpg

☐ Link external

Select this file | Cancel

We can resize its dimensions through the **Appearance** tab if we need to. We then click on **Insert** and it's done.

Have a go hero – add an image to your HTML block

Remember our **Welcome** block? If you click on the editing icon there, Moodle will operate in exactly the same way as it does with the topic summaries. Go back and insert an image there! (Again, not too large an image! For a block, I'd suggest 160 x 120 pixels). Then move the block so that it is positioned on the upper-left of our page, where the eye will naturally start reading from when a student enters the course. You should now have something like this:

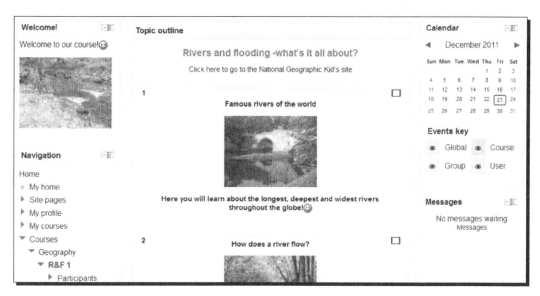

Compare this screenshot with our first view of the course page, as shown here:

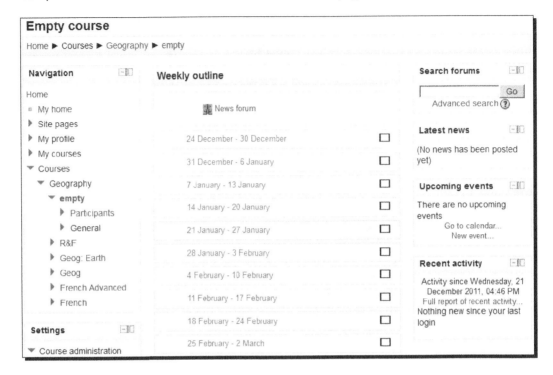

Better already!

If you want to get rid of **News forum**, as I have, then you need to change the number of news items to **0** in the course settings, in the **Administration** block. Then, with the editing turned on, click on the **X** icon next to **News forum**, to delete it.

Adding links to other websites in Moodle

Did you notice that I made a click here in **Topic 0** that links to **National Geographic Kids' site**? This is a really useful feature of Moodle, as it saves you from having to write a website on the board or in a worksheet, and it saves your students having to copy it, and then retype it when they get it wrong. One click and they're there! Let's end our introductory tour of our Moodle course by adding a relevant website link (or hyperlink).

Time for action – making a click here link to a website

There are two ways in which we can link to other websites in Moodle. For now, we're going to use the text editor and make a link in one of our topic summaries.

1. Turn on editing, and then click on the editing icon in one of the topic summaries.

2. Type in some text.

3. Select the text that you want the students to click on to go to your chosen website (It doesn't have to say *click here*—it can say anything you want).

4. Click on the chain icon, as shown in the following screenshot:

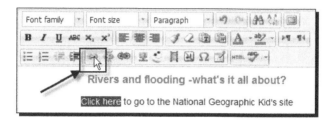

5. In the box that is displayed next, type in (or copy-and-paste) the URL of the website that you want them to visit, next to **Link URL**. (If you copy-and-paste, make sure that you only have *http://* at the start).

6. Next to **Title**, enter the name of the site, which will be seen when students hover their cursor over the link.

7. Make sure that **Target** specifies new window.

8. Click on **Insert**.

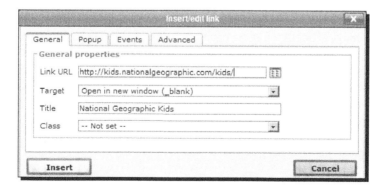

9. Back in the text editor, scroll down and click on **Save changes**.

What just happened?

Selecting some text (for example, **Click here**) and clicking on the chain icon enabled us to link directly to a useful site for our students. Choosing new window means that the site will open in a pop-up window. The children can close it with the **X** and will still have Moodle open on their screen. If you test it out yourselves, you'll see what I mean. The linked site can be resized and moved around, without losing Moodle.

Another neat feature for us to take advantage of!

Summary

In this chapter, we got to know our new Moodle course page and started customizing it with ready-to-add materials and student activities. We discussed how to alter the layout to suit our subject, students, and teaching style. We also looked at how to move and add useful blocks on either side of the main work area, learned how to add text and images to our course page to make it more attractive to young children, and how to add clickable links to external websites from our course.

There is nothing magical about what we have achieved so far—it's all very basic. Just think which website would your young students would be more inclined to visit and linger on—a bare page with a list of numbered topics waiting for an even longer list of Word-processed documents, or a bright, colorful website that is full of potential, waiting for the fun, resources, and activities that we will produce in the following chapters? Style over content? We've got the style—now let's get some content!

Adding Worksheets and Resources **2**

This chapter is all about saving energy. Not only our own, but the world's too! Moodle's main attraction, to many teachers, is the fact that you can upload all of those worksheets that you hand out in class (and that your students lose). When you've done it once, they are there for as long as you need them—so you don't have to find and print them off the next time you do that topic, and fewer trees will be felled in the name of education! We're teaching the topic of Rivers and Flooding; so to start with, we'll need to introduce our class to some basic facts about rivers and how they work. We aren't going to generate any new stuff yet; we're just going to upload to Moodle what we have already produced in previous years.

In this chapter, we shall:

- Put an information sheet about the River Thames into Moodle
- Load a whole week's slideshows about River processes into Moodle in a neat folder
- Make a **click here** type link (this is known as a **hyperlink**) to the **River Thames** website
- Create a worksheet about flooding by typing it straight into Moodle
- Insert an online movie from YouTube in a simple click of a button
- Make our page a bit prettier, now that we've got some real stuff on it

Putting a worksheet on Moodle

The way Moodle works is that we upload our worksheet to the central section of our course page, and it appears as a link for our students to click on. We've got an introductory factsheet (done in Word) about the River Thames. Let's get it into Moodle.

Time for action – uploading a factsheet on to Moodle

We need to get the worksheet uploaded into Moodle. To do this, we have to follow a few simple steps.

1. Go to your course page and click on the **Turn editing on** button, as shown in the following screenshot:

    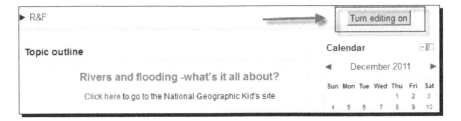

2. Don't worry about all of the new symbols (icons) that appear. In the section you want the worksheet to be displayed in, look for these two boxes:

3. Click on the **Add a resource...** box (I'll go through all its options when we have a recap, later).

4. Select **File**.

5. In **Name**, type the text that you want the students to click on, and in **Description** add a short description. (Depending on your Moodle admin, you might be able to leave this out or you might have to add one). Check the box **Display description on course page** if you want your description to be shown. The following screenshot gives an example of this:

6. Once you're done with the previous steps, click on **Add**. This takes you to what Moodle calls the **File picker**.

File picker is basically a screen with links on the left side. These take you to places where you can get your documents—or images, sounds, or videos—to add to your course. The links you see depend on what your Moodle admin has allowed for your school.

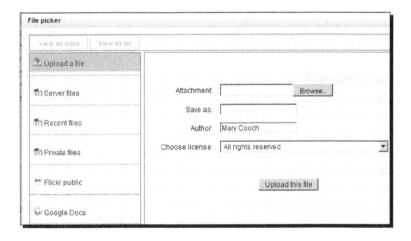

7. Click on **Upload this file**, and then click the **Browse** or **Choose file** button to browse your computer or USB drive to find the worksheet you want to upload.

8. Find the worksheet, select it with your cursor and click **Open**. It will appear in the box to the right of **Attachment**.

> You don't need to **Save as** anything else. (We want to save time.)
>
> You don't have to add the author. (We want to save time.)
>
> You can **Choose a license** or leave this step out—your students can still see your worksheet. (We want to save time.)

9. Click **Upload this file**. Once the file has been uploaded, it will appear as shown in the following screenshot:

10. This tells us that Moodle has uploaded our worksheet to this section of the course page.

11. Ignore (for now!) all the other settings. Scroll down and click **Save and return to course**.

What just happened?

Congratulations! You've now made a link to the factsheet about the River Thames that will get our **Rivers and Flooding** course started! By doing the previous final step, we will be taken back to the course page where we'll see the words that we wrote in the **Name** box. They'll be in blue. This tells us that it's a clickable link that will take us to the factsheet. If you can do that once, then you can do it many times.

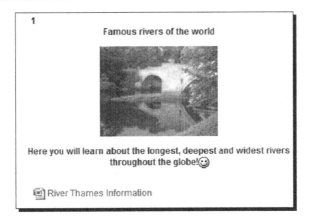

Have a go hero – putting a slideshow onto Moodle

It's important to go through the steps again, pretty quickly, so that you become familiar with them and are able to speed the process up. So why not take one of your slide shows (maybe done in PowerPoint) and upload that to Moodle?

Easy! But what exactly was that **File picker** we met along the way? Let's take a closer look as it offers a lot of possibilities for getting stuff from places other than our own computer.

What can you pick from the File picker?

The next screenshot shows a typical view of some links in the **File picker**:

The proper name for these links is **repositories**, but I like to think of them as a "lucky dip" can into which you can dig one of those long-handled pincers tools to get out a file of your choice.

There are many repositories you can have in the list. Your admin decides which ones your Moodle will use and Moodle itself is clever enough to know which ones are useful to you as well. If you want to add an image, for instance, it will show you Flickr or Picasa Web Albums. If you want to add a movie, it will show you YouTube. You can completely ignore them all if you simply want to upload files as we did just now, but just in case you are interested, here's a table of some of the most common repositories you might see and what they do.

Name of repository	What it does
Upload a file	Click this one to get to your own stuff on your computer.
Server files	Click here to look in other courses you're a teacher in to grab stuff to add to your present course.
Recent files	Click here to get back the last 50 or so files you've uploaded.
Private files	Click here to display, on your course page, a file you uploaded to your private files area (see *Chapter 1, Getting Started*).
Flickr Public	Click here to search Flickr for a publicly available photo as we did in *Chapter 1, Getting Started*.
Flickr	Click here to search your own Flickr account for a photo.
YouTube	Click here to search for and display a movie from YouTube. We will try this out later in the book!
Google docs	Click here to get a file from your own Google docs account.
Legacy course files	Click here to get files from a shared teacher course files area. (This tends to be only for old Moodles as it doesn't work very well).

If you want to know more about repositories, check out the documentation on the main worldwide Moodle site `http://docs.moodle.org/en/ Repositories`. It's been written for people with no technical background and is very easy to follow. In fact, there is a whole lot of free documentation on `http://docs.moodle.org` which you can refer to if you need more detail than this book gives. Check with your admin which exact version of Moodle you have, so you can choose the right documentation.

Putting a week's worth of slideshows into Moodle

Now, let's suppose that we have already prepared a week's worth of slideshows. Actually, I could say, a month's worth of worksheets, or a year's worth of exam papers. Basically, what we're going to do is upload several items, all at once. This is very useful because once you get used to uploading and displaying worksheets, you will very quickly start thinking about how tedious it would be to put them on Moodle one at a time. Especially if you are studying 10 major world rivers, and you have to go through all of those steps 10 times. Well, you don't!

Let's use my **River Processes** slideshows as our example. I have them saved in a folder on **My Computer** (as opposed to being shoved at random in a drawer, obviously!). Under normal circumstances, Moodle won't let you upload whole folders just like that. You have to either compress or zip them first (that basically means squeeze it up a bit, so it slides into cyberspace more smoothly).

We first need to leave Moodle for a while and go to our own computer. I'm using Windows; if you are using a Mac, you may have a slightly different view of the system.

Time for action – getting a whole folder of work into Moodle in one go

To view the slideshows, we need to upload the folder containing them from the hard drive of our computer into Moodle.

1. Find the folder that you want to upload, right-click on it, and select **Compressed (zipped) folder** within the **Send to** option.

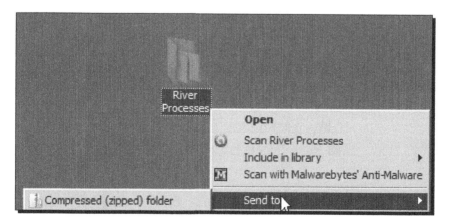

2. You'll get another folder with the same name, but in a ZIP format.

3. Go to your Moodle course page, turn on the editing as before, and in the section where you want to show this folder, click the **Add a resource...** drop-down menu and click on **Folder**:

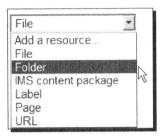

4. As we have done before, add **Name** (which makes the link that the children click on) and **Description**, checking the box if you want that description to show on the course page.

5. Now, click on **Add** as we did before to get to **File picker**.

6. Browse for and upload the folder which ends in `.zip` (The original one just won't work!) It will look like the following screenshot. Note the little icon to the right of the name. I have highlighted it in a square:

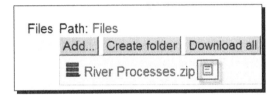

7. For our students to be able to see the slideshows properly, we have to "unzip" the folder and get it back to its original state. Click on that little icon to the right of the folder name and click on **Unzip**.

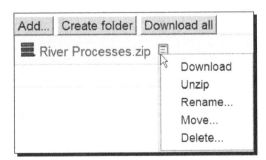

8. The folder will then appear in its normal form, which is what we want!

9. To get rid of the zipped folder, click that icon again and this time choose **Delete**:

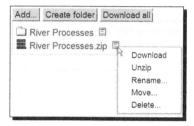

10. With our folder uploaded and unzipped, we're ready to go! Ignore the other settings (for now). Scroll down and click **Save and return to course**.

What just happened?

We put a bunch of slideshows about how rivers work into a folder on our computer. We then zipped the folder to make it slide into Moodle, and then when it was uploaded, we unzipped it to get it back to normal.

Instead of the icon of a slideshow, such as a PowerPoint icon, we get a folder icon. When our students click on it, the folder opens and all of the slideshows inside it can be viewed. It is much easier on the eye than going through a long list of stuff on the course's main page.

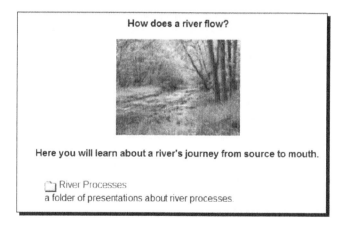

 Did you notice, as we uploaded the folder, that we had the option to create a folder? If you prefer, you can make an empty folder and then upload your slideshows into it one at a time—but it will take you longer!

Making a 'click here' type link to the River Thames website

Let's learn how to create a link that will lead us to the **River Thames** website or in fact to any website. However, we're investigating the Thames at the moment, so this would be really helpful. Just imagine, how much simpler it would be for our students to be able to get to a site in one click, rather than type it by hand, spell it wrong, and have it not work. We already learned one way to do this in *Chapter 1, Getting Started*. The way we will learn now is even easier than that. In fact, it's so easy that you could do it yourself with only a couple of hints from me.

Have a go hero – linking to a website

Did you know that the proper name for a web address is URL? With your editing turned on, go to the section you want your web link to be and from the **Add a resource** drop-down menu choose **URL**. Add **Name** and **Description** as before and in the box **External URL**, type (or copy and paste) the full address of the website you want to link to:

In the **Display** box, I'd choose **New window** because then the website will open in a pop-up window and when your students have finished, they've still got Moodle in the background:

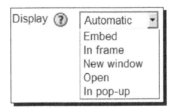

(If you don't have the **New window** option, ask your Moodle admin to switch it on).

That's it! Try it! Go back to your course page, click on the words that you specified as **Name** for the web page link, and check whether it works.

Recap—where do we stand now?

We have learnt a lot of interesting things so far. Let's just have a recap. We now know how to:

- Upload and display individual worksheets (as we've worked on the River Thames)
- Upload and display whole folders of worksheets (as we did with the **River Processes** slideshows folder)
- Make a **click here** type link to any website that we want, so that our students will just need to click on this link to get to that website

We're now going to have a break from filling up our course for a while, and take a step to the side. Our first venture into Moodle's features was the **File** option, but there are many more yet to be investigated. Let's have a closer look at those **Add a resource...** options in the following screenshot, so that we know where we are heading:

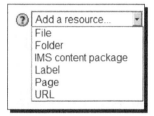

The following table shows all of the **Add a resource...** options. What are they, which is the one we need, and what can we safely ignore? You might recognize one or two already. We shall meet the others in a moment.

Item	What it is	Do we need it?
File	Shows our worksheet or slideshow.	Yes—we use it all the time.
Folder	Shows a whole folder.	Yes—makes the course page neater
IMS content package	A place to upload special types of resources (for advanced users).	No—but if you're curious, you can check out the info on Moodle: `http://docs.moodle.org/en/IMS_content_package.`
Label	A bit of white space to separate resources on the page.	Yes—it improves the appearance of the course page.
Page	Space to type straight into Moodle (and do more advanced stuff).	Yes—we can do our worksheets directly in Moodle with multimedia!
URL	A way to make a click here link to a website.	Yes—very useful.

Making a multimedia worksheet about flooding, directly in Moodle

Now, this is progress. At the start of the chapter, we had barely learned how to upload what we already had, and now we are thinking of typing straight into Moodle. But hold on—why should we bother? We're pretty proficient in MS Word, and with each upload we do, we take less time to do it.

Remember the introduction, where I said that this chapter was about saving energy—ours and the world's. Actually, it can also be about saving the children's energy, and even avoiding their frustration. If we go back to our course page and click on one of our worksheets, what happens? Depending on the browser that is being used—in this case **Internet Explorer** (**IE**)—we get a pop-up dialog box, as shown in the following screenshot:

Here, having already clicked on the link, we are being asked to make a choice between three options. If we choose **Open**, we will have to wait for a while, for the file to open. So that's two clicks and a wait. For a 10 year old, or even younger, that's a long time to wait, and the novelty will soon wear off once the kid's done that half a dozen times, once for each of our river's worksheets. Additionally, not all children have Microsoft Office installed (as we are going to see later, in *Chapter 8, Practicalities*), but they can all click a link on the Internet. So, can we not just have one click, and no wait?

Yes! If we type our worksheet straight into Moodle, as we're about to do. The next stage of our unit of work is to research the major floods that took place in the tiny Cornish village of Boscastle in 2004. Instead of wasting time typing a worksheet out and then uploading it, let's just do it in Moodle straight away, and cut out that middle step! And the big advantage of doing it directly into Moodle is that we can also add other cool stuff!

Time for action – typing our flooding worksheet straight into Moodle

We have already learned how to create worksheets and upload a folder containing them into Moodle. Let's now try to create a worksheet in Moodle, directly—but with an added twist!

1. With the editing turned on, go to **Add a resource** and click on **Page**.

2. In the **Name** field, type the text that the students will have to click on to access the page and in **Description** explain what it's about. Then, scroll down to the **Content** section.

3. Type in the instructions, as you would have done in Microsoft Word, or a similar software application.

4. Use the toolbar in the text editor to change the font size, color, and add images, according to your choice. It might look something like the following screenshot:

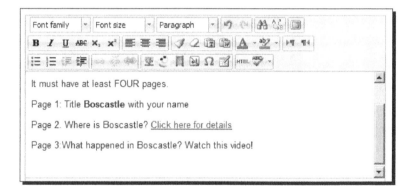

5. Before saving, let's do something really clever! Click the filmstrip (Moodle media) icon as in this screenshot:

6. On the next screen, click on the **Find or upload a sound, video or applet** button.

7. Click the **Youtube videos** link from the **File picker**.

8. In the **Search videos** box, type **Boscastle floods 2004** and then hit the **Search** button.

9. A load of YouTube videos about the floods will appear. Click the one you want!

10. On the next screen, click **Select this file**.

11. On the next screen, where you'll see it previewed, click **Insert**.

12. On the next screen, you'll just see a blue link and no video—but don't panic!

13. Click on **Save and return to course**.

What just happened?

We have now created our first worksheet directly in Moodle, without the need to create it offline first, and then upload it onto Moodle. And, we added a video for our students to learn from without needing to know any fancy web coding! (Note: if you don't see the video, ask your admin to turn on the "multimedia plugin filter").

If we go back to our course page and click on the words we used as **Name** we get to see the instructions and the video in just one click. Students will thank you for this, and you will be glad that you didn't have to type it out first and then upload it!

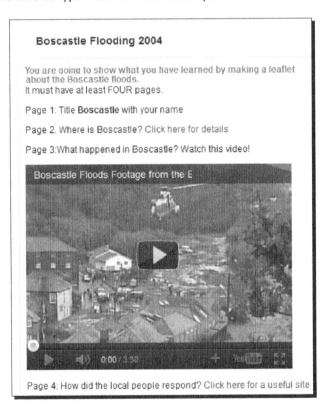

A word of warning about YouTube

If your school has banned YouTube, then your students won't be able to see the movie in school—although they can watch it at home. We'll look at how to get round this later in the book.

Online worksheets—some ideas to consider

I hope you can see that although being able to display a year's worth of worksheets and slideshows (which is a very powerful feature of Moodle) is useful, it can often be simpler and friendlier to create the task directly in Moodle. If you've already prepared a worksheet, for example in MS Word, you can also copy and paste it (although it doesn't always display exactly the same as your original).

If you are lucky enough to have a projector, a whiteboard, and an Internet connection in your room, why not present your instructions to your class on a web page in Moodle, instead of writing them by hand? You can then plan the course in advance and show it through your projector when you are ready.

If you have a homework task that does not involve the class having to download and take printouts of your worksheet, why not make that a web page?

If you can get your class into a computer room, why not have them view your web page on their own computers and follow the instructions there? These days, many schools are moving towards using laptops, or cute little netbooks or iPads for each child. We could well see Moodle as the virtual online exercise book of the future! You could use the hyperlinking facility to great advantage if you want them to do some research on a particular topic and need to guide them to specific areas. You provide them with the most useful websites, they click on your links, and they are now ready to begin their research! This is particularly helpful for younger children who need clear direction rather than simply "go to Google and research...".

Be careful that you avoid the usage of plain black text and long instructions. Adding movies is a great asset. Use different colors, bearing in mind any color blindness or visual impairments of your students. Brighten the page up with an image. (We looked at the display of images in *Chapter 1*, *Getting Started*).

Making our page look prettier

Is this really important? Shouldn't we be getting on with all of the other activities that Moodle can offer? Yes we should, and we shall, but it is vital that we make our course page appeal to the students. I cannot stress this enough. We have looked at this in *Chapter 1*, *Getting Started*, when we set our course up, and now that we've got topics with worksheets, folders, hyperlinks, and web pages that are starting to fill the screen space, it's worth looking at it again. We really need to ensure that our classes don't just take one look and run. Long pages of writing are sure to turn the users off.

How do you think the users might react to a Moodle page that appears as shown in the following screenshot?

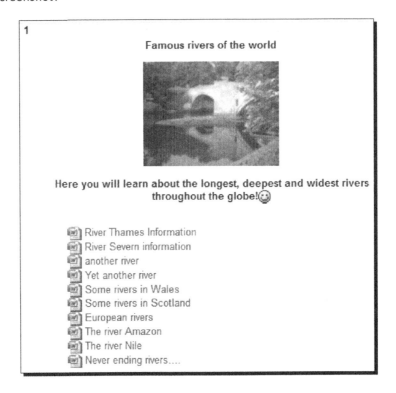

Even though it looks like a nice picture, the arrangement of the worksheets doesn't seem very pleasant to the eyes. We can do two things to improve it:

- Put them into a folder and show only that folder (**Folder**)
- Add a bit of white space between the worksheets to separate them, categorize them (and of course, give them more descriptive titles rather than **another river** and so on!)

We already know how to do the first option (but we must be careful, once we get loads of content in our course, that we don't just have long lists of folders instead of individual worksheets). So let's try the second option—the white space. We'll be using the **Label** that we saw in that table I made earlier.

Time for action – improving the look of our course page

Currently, our course page doesn't look very pleasant to the eye. Let's make it a little more interesting.

1. With editing turned on, go to **Add a resource** and choose **Label**.

2. Type in some text in order to separate or categorize a number of worksheets:

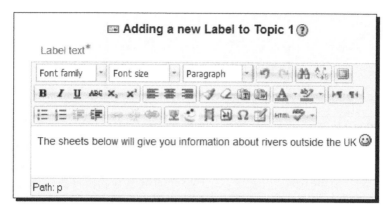

3. Finally, click on **Save and return to course**.

What just happened?

We added a description of the worksheets in the provided white space known as **Label**. It seems to be very nice, but the description has appeared underneath the names of the rivers when we wanted it in between. Check out the icons next to each of the resources when editing is turned on. They all have an important role to play in editing the material on our page:

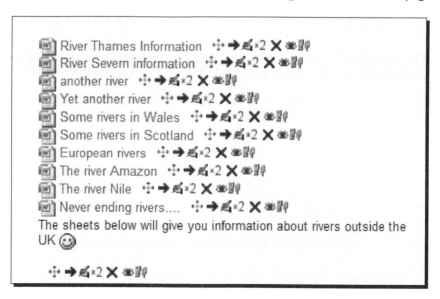

One of the listed icons will enable us to move the label to where we want it (by default, every time you add a resource on a Moodle page, it goes under the previous one). Here is a table that briefly explains what each icon does. Look out for the one that will move our label up.

Icon	What it is	Why do we need it?
1	Moves up or down	Very useful (you might have up/down arrow instead)
2	Indents to the right	For subsections/subheadings
3	Editing text	Essential for setting up/altering resources
4	Duplicating	Handy for making a copy of a resource to edit
5	Delete	Deletes your resource or activity
6	Hides item (click to close the eye; click again to re-open)	Very useful for showing an item only when you want to
7	Assign roles	Lets us give privileges to certain users—not something we need to worry about

Now, what we need is the crosshairs icon. You might have an up/down arrow icon on your Moodle instead. In this case, you click the icon and then click into an empty box where you want to move your label.

Have a go hero – move the label!

Just click on the crosshairs icon next to the label. Hold on and drag it to where you want and then let go:

Incidentally, we aren't tied to moving stuff within a topic area. We can move from one topic section to another and, in fact, use the arrows to the right of each topic section to move entire topics up and down.

You can get a preview of how the course page will appear to the student.

There's a useful link in the **Settings** block, called **Switch role to**. If you click on it and choose **Student**, it temporarily lets you see the page as the child would see it. Our latest effort would appear as shown in the following screenshot:

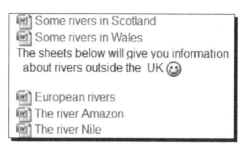

Summary

In this chapter, we've started assembling work for our classes in Moodle. We've looked at saving time and energy by getting individual worksheets into Moodle for our students (so we don't have to keep printing them, getting whole folders of work into Moodle (instead of uploading them one at a time), making quick and easy links to websites, creating a worksheet from scratch in Moodle, instead of doing this offline and then uploading the worksheet, and finding an easy way to show online videos to help our students' learning.

Additionally, we've also provided tips on improving the appearance of the course by showing work in a folder instead of showing everything separately in a list, breaking up the work into chunks by using a label, and moving items around the page.

Setting up that page was just the beginning. If we can do that, it's only one tiny step further to getting our students to learn interactively and to send us their work within Moodle. That's where we're heading in the next chapter.

3
Getting Interactive

Congratulations on reaching Chapter 3! Some people choose never to go beyond the skills acquired in Chapters 1, Getting Started, and Chapter 2, Adding Worksheets and Resources, and are then surprised when their Moodle course doesn't really take off with the students or their colleagues. In the following pages, we shall reach into the heart of Moodle. The previous chapters were about what we could do for our children. This one is about what they can give back to us!

This chapter combines classroom tasks with Moodle activities, in a mini project that will get our students to think and collaborate. We'll also add a competitive element to it and—just as we have seen on TV—let the children vote for the winner. The tasks we set will involve the students researching, collaborating, and reflecting. They will be working hard, but we'll have a much easier time now, as all of their responses will be on Moodle for us to view and mark at our convenience—no more carrying heavy books around.

We are going to carry out a role-play activity. This activity will be geography based, but the Moodle activities are the same for any subject. Hopefully, this will help you gain some ideas for your own teaching. Having learned about the course of a river and about the landscape at the location where the river meets the coast, the students are now going to be given the job of developers—planning and designing a riverside campsite. The students will undertake various tasks during the project, all of them within Moodle. We, the teachers, having set the scene, are going to sit back and observe their progress online. When the entire mini project is complete, we're going to get them to tell us, personally, how much they feel they have learned. We can use their responses to plan our future Moodle activities.

In this chapter, we shall encourage our students to join in by:

♦ Allowing them to discuss the considerations in choosing the location of this campsite in a safe, moderated **forum**

♦ Giving them an out-of-school hours chat room in which they can plan their site

♦ Asking them to suggest creative names for the site and entering these names in a class **glossary**

♦ Providing a space (in a **database**) to send in their designs for the teacher to assess and their classmates to view

♦ Letting the class vote on the winner and evaluate the project by using a Moodle **choice**

♦ Getting them to send in their advert for us to mark directly within Moodle as an **assignment**

♦ Having them tell a story to which everyone can contribute by using a **Wiki**

How do we do all this?

The words in **bold** above are examples of activities that we can do in Moodle. There are others too, but for you—as a newbie—these seven activities are more than enough. To set up any of them, we first need to turn editing on, either via the button on the upper-right of the screen, or via the **Course administration** link in the **Settings** block.

Then, in the topic section where we want to add our activity, we click on the space next to **Add an activity**. This will bring up a list of options, which might vary depending upon your particular Moodle course. The following screenshot shows some typical options that might show up when you click on **Add an activity**:

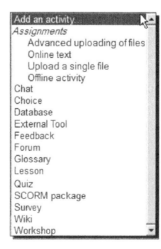

Getting our class to reflect and discuss

Have you ever come across a child who is too shy to speak up in class but then produces the most thoughtful written work? Moodle is perfectly suited to these students, because it has a **Forum** and a **Chat** facility, both of which enable classes and their teachers to have a discussion without actually being together, in the same room. And often, the shy child will happily have their say online, where they can plan it out first and feel comfortable without the interference of their peers.

We're going to set some homework where the students will discuss, in general, the kinds of things to keep in mind when planning a riverside campsite. Hopefully, someone will realize it's not a good idea to have it too close to the water.

Time for action – setting up a discussion forum on Moodle

Let's create an online discussion area for the students to share their views and comments. This discussion area is called the **Forum**.

1. With editing turned on, click on **Add an activity** and select **Forum**.

2. In the **Forum type** field, click on the drop-down arrow and choose **A single simple discussion** (we'll investigate the other options later).

3. In the **Forum name** field, enter some text that will invite your students to click on it to join the discussion.

4. In the **Forum introduction** field, enter your starting topic, with images and hyperlinks if you wish.

5. If you want the description displayed on the course page, check the box **Display description on course page**. Here's a screenshot of where we are so far:

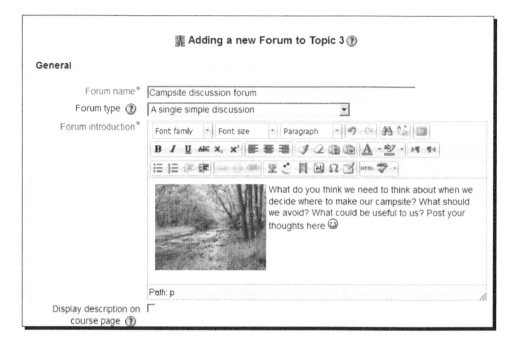

6. Change the option **Force everyone to be subscribed** to **Yes**, if you want people to get an e-mail every time somebody adds their comments or suggestions to the forum.

7. Leave the option **Read tracking** as it is, and people can decide whether to track read or unread messages.

8. The option **Maximum attachment size** lets you decide how big a file or an image people can attach with a message and **Maximum number** is how many they can attach.

9. Grade—If you turn **Ratings** on in the next section, you'll then be able to alter these **Grade** settings to give each post a mark. But, be aware that this could put younger children off. I don't do it.

10. You can put a number in the **Post threshold for blocking** option if you want to limit the number of posts that a student can make.

11. Ignore any other settings (it's quite safe!) and click **Save and return to course**.

What just happened?

We have just set up an online discussion area (**Forum**) on a specific topic for our class. Let's go back to our course page and click on the forum that we just prepared. The final output will look like this to a student (as you can see, if you click on **Switch role to student** in the **Settings** block):

Our students will see an icon (usually with two faces) that will prompt them to join the preliminary discussion on where best to locate the campsite. They'll click on the **Reply** link at the bottom-right to post their response.

How do we moderate the forum?

Hopefully, we can just read the students' responses and let them discuss the topic among themselves. But as a teacher, we do have four other options:

1. We can edit the response posted by the student (change the wording if it's inappropriate).

2. We can delete the post altogether.

3. We can move an inappropriate post to a hidden "quarantine" forum so that our head teacher and the child's parent can see exactly what was posted. (If you think you might need this, check out the documentation here: `http://docs.moodle. org/22/en/Forum_FAQ`.)

4. We can reply to it when we think it is really important to do so.

A student only has the option to reply (although they can edit or delete their entry within a short period after posting.) When we need to get rid of an unsuitable post, or perhaps alter the wordings of something one of our students has typed, this extra power, that we teachers have, is helpful.

For our starter discussion, we chose **A single simple discussion** as we wanted the students to focus totally on one issue. However, in other situations, you might need a slightly different type of forum. So the following table gives a brief overview of the other kinds that are available, and explains how you could use them:

Name	What it does	Why use it
A single simple discussion	Only one question students can all answer	Best for focused discussions—students can't get distracted
Standard forum	Everyone can start a new topic	More scope for older students
Standard forum in blog-like format	Everyone can start a new topic	For older students who are used to commenting on blogs
Q and A	Pupils must answer first before they can see any replies	Useful for avoiding peer pressure issues
Each person posts 1 discussion	Pupils can post one new topic only	Handy if you need to restrict posting but still allow some freedom

Why use a forum?

Here are a few other thoughts on forums, based on my own experiences:

◆ A cross-year or cross-class forum can be useful, as the older students can pass on their experiences to the younger students. For example, each year my first year high school students make a volcano as a homework project. As they enter their second year, they use a dedicated forum to pass on their wisdom and answer technical questions sought by the inexperienced first-year students—who are about to begin their own creations.

◆ A homework exercise could be set on a forum, as a reflective plenary to the learning done in the class. Once, my class watched a documentary based on the Great New Orleans flood of 2005, and the students were asked, on a forum, to imagine they had been there. They had to suggest some words or phrases to describe their feelings—which we then collated into the next lesson to make poems about the flood.

Let's add a little bit of confusion. Instead of simply asking a question, why not make a statement that you know will inspire, annoy, and divide the students. As a result, you can see the variety in the responses. I once posted the topic: *If people live near rivers, and their homes get flooded out, it is surely their own fault for living near rivers. Why should the rest of us have to help them?* In response to this, some violently disagreed with the statement—quoting examples from developing countries— whereas some agreed with the statement and were then blasted down by their classmates for doing so. (Best to keep an eye on the forum for any possible bullying.) But, at least the forum got visited!

Carrying on the conversation in real time—outside of school

A discussion forum, as illustrated previously, is a useful tool to get the children to think and to contribute their ideas. It has an advantage over the usual class discussion, in that the shyer pupils are more likely to open up in such discussion forums. However, there is no spontaneity involved. You might post a comment in the morning, and the response may arrive at dinner time, and so on.

Why not combine the advantages of online communication with the advantages of a real time conversation, and make a **Moodle chat room**? If your students live several miles away from each other, as my students do, and are keen to get on with the project, Moodle chat rooms can have real benefits. We can set a time for the chat—say, Saturday afternoon. This would be a time when we can be present too, if we wish, and the students can move ahead with their plans even though they're not with each other in the classroom. Even though this implementation has its own drawbacks, it provides us with a set-up. We can see how it goes and then think about how best we can use it.

Time for action – setting up a chat room in Moodle

Let's set up a chat room in our **Rivers and Flooding** course so that our students can discuss their plans:

1. With editing turned on, go to **Add an activity**, and select the **Chat** option.

2. In the **Name of this chat room** field, enter an appropriate title for the discussion.

3. In the **Introduction text** field, type in what the discussion is going to be about. If you want this to show on the main course page, check the box **Display description on the course page**.

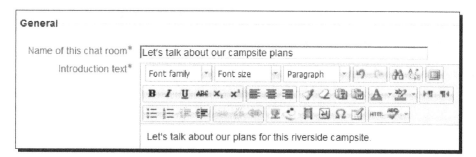

4. For the **Next chat time** option, choose when you want to open the chat room.

5. For the **Repeat sessions** option, choose whether you want to chat regularly or just once.

6. For the **Save past sessions** option, choose how long, if at all, to keep a record of the conversation. (This might be useful if you won't be present at the chat or else if the chat will form part of an assessed task.)

    It is up to you to decide whether to allow everyone to view the past sessions or not.

7. Ignore all other settings!

8. Click on **Save and display**.

What just happened?

We have set up the place and time on Moodle for our students to talk to each other—and even with us if necessary—online. Students will see an icon—often a speech bubble—on the course page, alongside the name given to the chat. The students just have to click on the icon at the correct time for the chat and they will see this:

Clicking on the link will take the students to a box where they'll be able to see their user photo (if they have one) and the time at which they have entered the chat. When others join in, their photos will be shown, and the time of their arrival will be recorded.

You talk by typing into the long box at the bottom of the screen, and when submitted, your words appear in the larger box above it. This can get quite confusing if a lot of people are typing at the same time, as the contributions appear one under the other, and do not always follow on from the question or response to which they are referring. If you have students with learning difficulties or conditions such as ADHD, they might not be able to make sense of the flow of a typical chat.

Why use chat? (and why not?)

Chat does have one advantage over the **Forum**, which is that you can hold discussions in real time with the others who are not physically present in the same room as you. This could be useful on occasions, such as when the teacher is absent from school (but available online). He or she can contact the class at the start of the lesson to check whether they know what they are doing.

The students in our school council use chat for meetings out of school hours, as do our school governors. You can also read the transcript of a chat (the chat log) after it has happened. However, everyone really has to stay focused on the discussion topic, otherwise, you risk having nothing but a list of trite comments, and no real substance. I've found this to be the case with younger children. Personally, I find a single and a simple discussion in a forum to be of much more value, than chat and I have to confess that I have switched off the ability for people to use **Chat** on my school's Moodle site. However, you can try using **Chat** and see what you think. Your experience could be different from mine.

Making our own class Glossary

Finally, the thinking part is over; now it's time to get started. Our campsite needs a name, and thirty heads are better than one. The next task will have the students suggesting interesting names for the site and the reasons why they think that their name should be chosen.

For this, we are going to use **Glossary**, which is similar to an online dictionary. The only difference is that it is you (or the students) who adds all the information into the **Glossary**. You can add single words, phrases, or even images to a glossary. You can even set it up in such a way that when you use one of the keywords in your course, Moodle automatically makes a link to the entry for that word in the glossary. The students can then click on these links to learn more about them.

Glossaries are useful for teachers who want to provide key terms for a particular topic, but students learn best from them when they build up the vocabulary themselves. We're going to get our students to add possible names for the riverside site to a **Glossary**. We want the students to think creatively and imaginatively, and to justify their choices.

Time for action – getting students to create their own Glossary

Let's create a **Glossary** where the students will be able post their suggestions. This will help us in understanding their choices.

1. With editing turned on, select the **Glossary** option, within the **Add an activity** option.

2. Provide a suitable name for the glossary in the **Name** field, and describe what the glossary's about in the **Description** text block. It might be a good idea here to explain how the students add entries, if they haven't used this feature before. If you want the description to show on the main course page, check the box **Display description on course page**.

3. There are many options that you can specify for a glossary. To start with, just leave them as they are shown in the following screenshot:

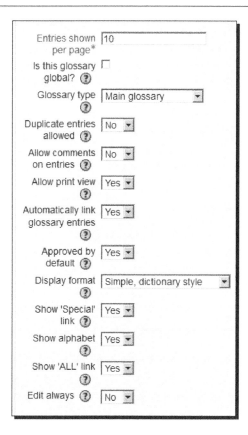

If you want to moderate entries before they appear in the glossary, choose **No** in the **Approved by default** field. If you want to let students comment on entries, choose **Yes** in the **Allow comments** on entries box.

4. Ignore all the other settings and click on **Save and display**.

What just happened?

We've set up an area in Moodle where our class students can add their suggested names for the campsite. We're using **Glossary** which we could—under other circumstances—use as a collaborative dictionary, giving our students the task of building it up, and saving ourselves the effort.

If we look at the finished article now, it will appear as shown in the following screenshot:

- ◆ In order to enter a word, or suggested campsite name into the glossary, click on **Add a new entry**
- ◆ In the **Concept** field, enter your word or term—in our case, the suggested campsite name
- ◆ In the **Description** field, enter the definition of the glossary term—in our case, the reason behind the choice of name

Don't be put off by all the tabs. As you get more into Moodle, you can investigate the glossary further. You can set categories for entries. For example, you can add keywords, that is, synonyms that will be hyperlinked to our glossary terms wherever they appear in our course.

We could also set a rating system for the glossary and allow our students to give points to the most popular names. For now, however, we just want our class to add words.

Showcasing the plans in a database

Let's assume that the students have decided on the campsite location and design. The students can make use of **Microsoft Paint** or **LibreOffice Draw** to draw and label their plans. They have to save their work as a .jpg file—in other words, as an image ready to be shared with others.

We now need a space on Moodle where the students can send in their plans for others to see and to vote for. In this case, a Moodle **database** will serve our purpose well.

Don't be put off by the term database. Being a non-technical person myself, the term database conjures up visions of complex formulae and spreadsheets to me. In Moodle, the database is merely a communal area where anyone can upload items or add information for others to view. However, as with the glossary, the Moodle database has a lot of extra features that we don't need yet—so we'll just ignore them.

Time for action – setting up a database

Let's create a database to which the students can post their designs.

1. With editing turned on, select the **Database** option within the **Add an activity** option.

2. In the **Name** field, provide a suitable title for your database.

3. In the **Introduction** block, specify what you want the students to add—in our case, the image file of their campsite design.

4. If you want this to show on the course main page, check the box **Display description on course page**.

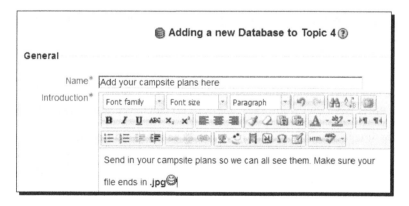

5. Don't worry about any settings that you're not sure of. For now, ignore them all and just click on **Save and display**.

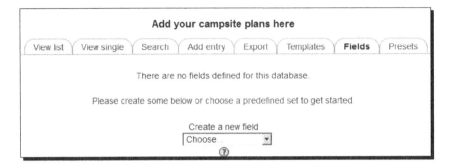

6. Click on the drop-down arrow for the **Create a new field** option, and select **Picture**, as shown in the following screenshot:

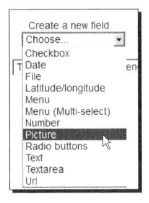

 Fields are simply bits of information, such as names, addresses, dates, and so on. Note that each field has to have a different name; you cannot have two the same.

7. In the **Field name** field, enter a suitable title for the field and in the **Field description** field, enter what you want the student to do (such as upload their campsite design).

8. Set the image size, if you wish, by entering a width and height in pixels next to the **Width** and **Height** fields. (**Single view** is when the picture is shown on its own and **List view** is when it is shown with others.)

9. Click on **Add**, and then from the **Create a new** field option select **Textarea**.

10. Fill in the appropriate details, as shown in the following screenshot, setting the width and height for the text field depending on the amount of text that you want the students to enter (you might need to experiment with an optimum text box size).

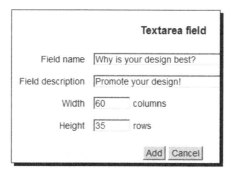

11. Click on the **Add** button to save.

What just happened?

We set up an area—a database—in Moodle with space for our students to send in their plans, and space for them to sell us their designs. If we look at our finished activity, we will see this:

Clicking on the **Add entry** tab will take us—and our students—to the upload area, as shown in the following screenshot:

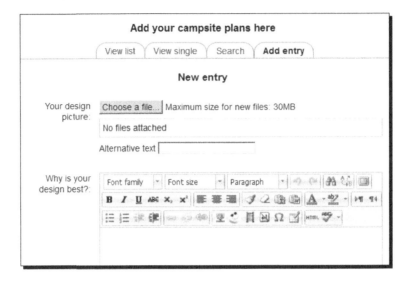

Now we need to wait until all the designs are in. Let's take a break for a moment.

How far have we come?

The aim of this chapter was to get our students involved—as our Teaching Assistant—in a project with Moodle. So far, they've made use of the **Forum** and the chat room to exchange their initial thoughts and ideas. They've come up with the names for the site, which they've shared in a glossary, and also come up with the actual design, which they have uploaded to a database.

They weren't tied to working in the classroom or during school hours. They didn't even need to be sitting side-by-side with their classmates to discuss. Just imagine, the students have set up the tasks, and they didn't even need us—the teachers—to be there (although it's important to keep an eye on their discussions).

This is another attraction of Moodle; students can work independently, once they have understood what is to be done. However, one thing that Moodle cannot do is choose the best campsite design (although, it can mark many other activities for us—as we shall see in *Chapter 4, Self-marking Quizzes*). Now, that we are done with our short break, let's add an option to our course page that enables our class to pick the winner.

Giving our class a chance to vote

Moodle has an activity, known as Moodle **Choice**, which allows you to present students with a number of options that they can choose from. We're actually going to use it twice in our project, for two different purposes. Let's us try and set it up.

Time for action – giving students a chance to choose a winner

The students have posted their suggestions, comments, and views on Moodle. A choice is to be made of the best suggestion. Who better than the students themselves to choose and vote for the best?

1. With editing turned on, click on **Add an activity** and then select **Choice**.

2. In the **Name** field, enter an appropriate descriptive text—in our case, this is **Vote for the best design here**.

3. In the **Choice text** field, ask the question based on what you want the students to cast a vote for. If you want this to show on the main course page, check the **Display description on course page** box.

4. Leave the **Limit** field as it is if you don't mind any number of students casting a vote for any option available. Change it to **enable**, if you only want a certain number of people to vote for a particular choice. We shall leave the **Limit** block as it is, but we shall inform the students that they can't vote for themselves.

5. In the **Options** boxes, type in the options (a minimum of two) you want the students to be able to cast their vote for. Clicking on **Add more fields** will provide you with more options boxes. We will need one field for each member of the class, for this activity.

6. Use the **Restrict answering to this time period** option to decide when to open and close your **Choice**—or have it always available.

7. Miscellaneous settings: For our activity, we need to set **Display Mode** to **Vertical** set and **Publish Results** to **Do Not Publish**. The following table explains what the settings mean, so you can use them on other occasions.

Setting	What it is	Why use it
Display Mode	Lets you have your buttons go across or down the screen	Use **Vertically** if you have many options, to avoid stretching your screen
Publish Results	Decide if and when you want students to see what others have specified	Choose **Do not publish** if you want students to tell you their progress privately; if you're doing a class survey, for example, choose **Always show results**
Privacy of Results	Lets you choose whether to show names or not	Are the results more important than who voted for what? Some students might be wary of responding if they think their names will be shown
Allow choice to be updated	Lets students change their mind—but they can still vote only once	Useful, if you are using this to assess progress over a period of time
Show column for unanswered	Sets up a column showing those who haven't yet responded	A clear visual way of knowing who hasn't done the task

8. Ignore all the other settings and just click on **Save and return to course**.

What just happened?

We've set up an area, on our course page, where the students can choose their favorite designs from a number of options by clicking on the desired option button. On the screen, you will be able to see an icon (usually, a question mark) and some text next to it. If your students click on the text next to the icon, the following information will appear:

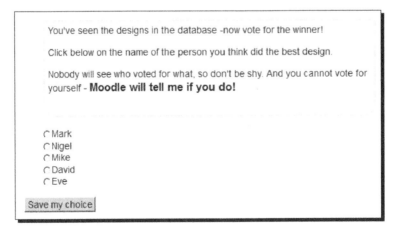

The students will click on the option button placed next to their choice—in our case, the name of the classmate whose design they prefer.

To find out the students' choice, follow these steps:

1. Access the **Choice** option and click on the words **View *** responses** on the upper-right of the screen. The *** will be the number of students who have voted already.

2. You will get a chart displaying the choices of the students. In my Moodle course, as shown in the following screenshot, **Mark** is clearly in the lead so far:

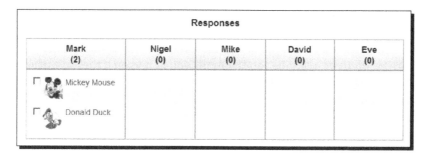

	Responses			
Mark (2)	Nigel (0)	Mike (0)	David (0)	Eve (0)
☐ Mickey Mouse				
☐ Donald Duck				

Remember that we have set up this activity so that our students cannot see the results, in order to avoid peer pressure or bullying. However, we can see the results. Thus, if Mickey votes for himself (even after having been told not to) we will spot it and can reprimand him.

Have a go hero – getting the class to give us feedback

After we've gone through all of the effort to set up our project on Moodle, it would be nice to know how well it was received. Why not go off now and set up another **Choice** option, where the question asks *How much did you enjoy planning and designing the campsite?* You could give them three simple responses (displayed horizontally) as:

1. A lot.

2. It was OK.

3. Not very much.

Or you could be more specific, focusing on the individual activities and asking how much they feel they have benefited from, say, the chat or the **Forum**. Make sure it is set up so that the students don't see the results—that way they're more likely to be truthful.

Why use Choice?

Here are a few other thoughts on **Choice**, based on my own experiences:

◆ It is a fast and simple method of gathering data for a class research project. I used this with a class of 13 year olds who had just returned from the summer break. I asked them to choose where they had been on vacation, giving them the choices of our own country, several nearby countries in Europe, the United States of America, and a few more. I set up the choice, so that they could all see the answers when the time was up. I also set it up in such a way that the results were anonymous, to avoid any kind of uneasiness felt by those students who had stayed at home. The class then compared and contrasted the class results with Tourist Office statistics on the most popular tourist destinations.

◆ It offers a private way for students to evaluate and inform the teacher about their progress. Students might be too shy to tell you in person if they are struggling; they might be wary of being honest in the open voting methods that some teachers use (such as red, amber, or green traffic lights). However, if the students are aware of the fact that their classmates will not see their response, they are more likely to be honest with you.

◆ It acts as a way to involve the class in deciding the path that their learning will take. I first introduced my class of 11 year olds to rivers in Europe, South America, Africa, and Asia. Then, I offered the class the chance to vote for the river that they wanted to study in greater depth as part of their project. The majority opted for the Amazon—so the Amazon it was!

Announcing the winner

Well, you could give out the results in the classroom, of course! Alternatively, we can encourage them to use Moodle by using the **Page** resource that we met in the previous chapter, and adding the information there.

Writing creatively in Moodle

Once a winner has been found, the next task for everyone is to create a cleverly-worded advertisement for this campsite, for which you could use one of the names suggested in the glossary. This too can be done on Moodle. Why use Moodle and not their exercise books?

The first reason is that it will save paper, the second reason is that the students enjoy working on the computer, and the third and final reason is that we can work at our leisure in school, at home, or in any room where there is an Internet connection. We're not tied to carrying around a pile of heavy books. We don't even need to manually hand-write the grades into our gradebook. Moodle will put the grades that we give our students, into its gradebook automatically and alphabetically.

Moodle can also send our pupils an e-mail telling them that we've graded their task, so that they can check their grades. This might be a different way of working from the one that you are used to, but do give it a try. It will take the pressure off your back and shoulders, if nothing else.

Time for action – setting up an online creative writing exercise

For our advert, we'll use an **Online text** assignment. We'll have a look at the others afterwards.

 In Moodle-speak, an assignment is a place where students can send you work. In the newest version of Moodle, due out in June 2012, the settings for assignments will change a little from those shown as follows. You will still be able to do all of our activities though, and if you need any extra guidance, check out the up-to-date documentation on `http://docs.moodle.org/Assignment`.

1. With editing turned on, select **Online text** from the **Add an activity** drop-down menu.

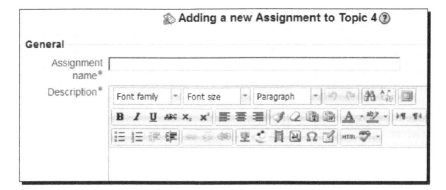

2. In the **Assignment name** field, enter something descriptive—our students will click here to get to the task.

3. In the **Description** field, enter the instructions. If you want them to appear on the main course page, check the **Display description on course page** box. Our screen will then appear as shown in the following screenshot:

 If you need more space to type in, click on the icon in the far-right of the top line of the text editor. This will enlarge the text box for you. Click it again when you're done, to return to the editing area.

4. In the **Grade** field, enter the total marks out of which you will score the students (for now, we're sticking to a maximum of 100, but you can change this).

5. Set a start and end date between which the students can send the work assigned to them, if you want.

6. Leave the **Prevent Late Submissions** option as it is, unless you need to set a deadline by which the students must submit the assigned work.

7. Set the **Allow Resubmitting** option to **YES**, if you want to let students redraft their work.

8. Set the **Email Alerts to teachers** option to **NO** (unless you want 30 emails in your inbox!).

9. Change the **Comment inline** option to **YES**, so that we can post a comment on the students' work.

10. Ignore all the other settings and click on **Save and return to course**.

What just happened?

We've just explained to our class what we want them to do, and have also provided them with space in Moodle to do it. We used an **Online text** assignment.

When our students click on the assignment icon (which is often a hand holding a piece of paper), there's a rather unfriendly command at the bottom of our assignment. Do you think that your students will know that they need to click here to get to their textbox?

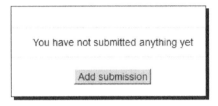

Why not ask your Moodle administrator to look at the **Language customization** settings and change these words to something more child-friendly—such as *Click this button to type your answer*?

Time for action – marking students' work on Moodle

Now that the students have done their bit, it's time that we did ours. The difference is that, instead of staying late after school or taking a pile of exercise books home and then searching around for a red pen (or green, as in my school) we can just type our comment on top of their entry.

1. Go back to the assignment and click on it.

2. Click the **View** *(number)* **submitted assignments** as shown in the following screenshot:

View 1 submitted assignments

SPARKLING, SIZZLING advert for the new

II this site to me!! Why should I go

se adjectives, adverbs and give it some

3. The number displayed on the screen is the number of children who've completed the task. Clicking on the link transports us to Moodle's online gradebook, as shown in the following screenshot:

4. We see who has handed in their work. Click on **Grade** for the student whose work you want to grade.(**Mickey Mouse**, in our case).

 Moodle has also recorded the time at which the student posted it, and will also record the time that we (the teacher) grade the post.

5. A window appears similar to the one shown in the following screenshot:

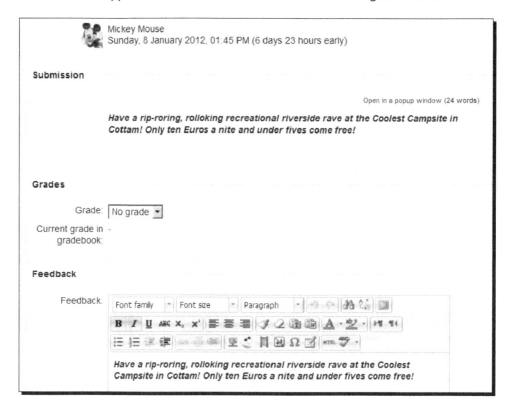

6. The student's effort is shown at the top of the screen—but, it's also present in our text editor box underneath. So, Mickey will always have the original to compare against our corrections. We can type a general comment, ahead of Mickey's work, using a different color to separate our work from his. We can then use the features of the text editor to highlight, cross out, or even underline errors, depending on our personal marking style.

Moodle also tells us how many words the student has written (in our case, 24 words). I have made it clear that I wanted the suggestion to be 100 words, so that's lost him some marks already.

7. Select a suitable grade in the box in the middle.

Before we save, let's just look at the corrected version. It will look similar to what is shown in the following screenshot:

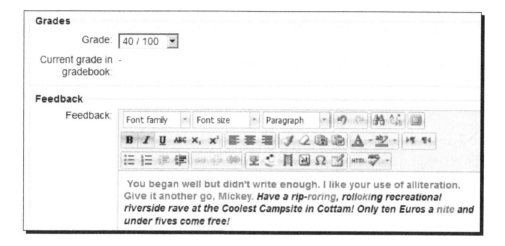

8. If we have lots to mark, we can click on **Save and show next**, which will take us to the next student's effort. Let's just click **Save changes** for now.

What just happened?

We have just finished grading the students on their very first exercise in Moodle! The gradebook was waiting there for us. We saw that **Mickey Mouse** had sent in his work. We clicked on **Grade** and were able to correct it, comment on it, and give it a grade. By saving our corrections, we've now added them to the gradebook and can see how this looks in the following screenshot:

However, for one thing, I need to chase up **Donald Duck** as he hasn't posted his suggestion yet! Mickey's grade is located along with the first part of my comments. He'll get an e-mail telling him to go and check his score. If I change my mind after I've marked others, I can always click on **Update**, and alter the student's grade.

> More than one teacher or class can work on the same assignment in Moodle and have them displayed separately. However, to implement this, you'll have to ask your Moodle administrator to set up groups for you. This isn't something we're looking at right now, but as you get more into Moodle, you'll find it a useful feature.

Other ways to set and mark work in Moodle

If you just want your students to perform a piece of writing, such as an advert, a letter, or a description, then the **Online text** assignment would be the best choice. But there might be times when the students need to actually upload files, such as presentations or leaflets that they have created.

Moodle has four types of assignments you can use (although one of them is a bit of a cheat, really as it isn't done inside Moodle). The following table explains the benefits of each one, so that you can select the one that is most suited to your purposes. (Remember that if you are using the newest version of Moodle after June 2012, you might see these presented slightly differently.)

Type of assignment	What it's for	Why use it
Online text	Allows students to type straight into Moodle, and allows teachers to correct online	For shorter passages of plain text, it's the quickest and simplest way to set and mark work
Upload a single file	Gives students the ability to upload a file, such as a Word-processed document or PowerPoint	For tasks that aren't suited to the online text type, say when you need to upload a certain file type such as a spreadsheet or slideshow
Advanced uploading of files	Students can send more than one item; teachers can return the corrected work for students to revise	If you like commenting on the students' work, but online text isn't for you, you can use this option to mark and return a Word-processed document; you can also use it if you are doing a project involving several pieces of work
Offline activity	Students produce work offline, such as a class role play, and it is marked in Moodle	This is just a space in Moodle's gradebook for you to record the marks for tasks done outside of Moodle

Have a go hero – mark their campsite design

It's now your turn! The students have uploaded the campsite designs to a database so that everyone can see them. Unfortunately, the designs are not linked to the gradebook. However, you could still mark each individual student by using the **Offline activity** facility. Why not set it up and see how the gradebook appears ready for you to mark the designs?

Collaborative story-telling

The project is nearly over, but as an entertaining plenary, let's get the students to put their minds and imaginations together to devise a spooky tale about a night on the campsite! We'll help to start them off, and then they can all join in by adding, editing (and even deleting) others' contributions. We shall use a Moodle **wiki** for this, as a wiki is a great tool for collaboration. However, like the glossary, and even the database, a wiki has many more features than we require at present. So we'll just stick to what we need.

Time for action – getting our class to work together on an online story

Let's make things more interesting! Let's ask the students to post an imaginative story.

1. With editing turned on, select the **Wiki** option within the **Add an activity** option.

2. In the **Wiki name** field, provide a suitable title for your wiki, and in the **Wiki description** field, enter a short explanation of what you want the students to add. If you want this to show on the main course page, check the **Display description on course page** box.

3. For the **Mode** option, choose **Collaborative** (we'll take a closer look at the other option later).

4. In **First Page Name**, give your story a title.

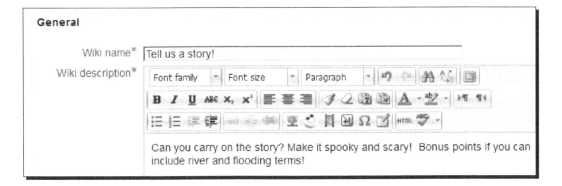

5. Don't worry about the settings that you don't understand. For now, just click on **Save and display**.

6. On the next screen, just click on **Create page**.

7. On the screen that is displayed next, enter the beginning of the story (or anything you want them to continue with) and click on **Save**.

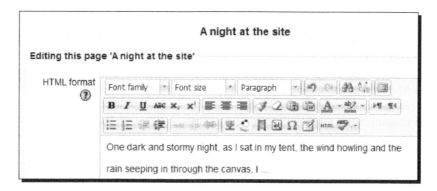

 You can add extra pages to a wiki by adding two square brackets around the name of the page that you type into the text editor. The next time that you save it, it will link to the new page. We're just going to have our story on one page, for the sake of simplicity.

What just happened?

The students now have, thanks to our efforts, a communal space on Moodle where they can continue the story. They can click on the wiki, enter the desired text into it, and save it, as they would do, if it were a **Forum** or an **Online text** assignment.

The benefit of our collaborative wiki is that our entire class can come to the same page and add, edit, and delete what has been entered. However, if we object to any student's act, we can click on **History** and see who did it, when they did it, and precisely what they did.

Although we chose **Collaborative** for our wiki, there is also an **Individual** wiki. This gives each student their own wiki to work on. This could be useful as an online exercise book for private notes or revision purposes.

Summary

In this chapter, we used Moodle activities to help us deliver a class project. The added benefit was that we could focus on getting our students to take control of their learning by getting them to think and reflect on their work in a safe and a moderated environment (using **Forum** and **Chat**), and by having them share ideas in a **Glossary** and present designs in a **Database**. We have also given them a chance to peer assess and offered them the opportunity to evaluate their progress privately (using **Choice**). They have been provided with an online space to perform a written task (using an **Assignment**) and have been encouraged to pool ideas and collaborate on a class story (using a **Wiki**).

Perhaps, now that we've got them engaged with Moodle, it is time to get some grades in our gradebook. The next chapter will teach us to set up interesting exercises for our class students. These exercises will not only be enjoyable for them, but will involve no marking at all on our part. Moodle will do it all for us. Interested? Read on!

4
Self-marking Quizzes

This chapter is all about work-life balance. This chapter will teach you how to introduce, practice, and consolidate learning in Moodle through the use of online activities such as quizzes, crosswords, and matching exercises. It will show you how, with the click of a button, you can have differentiated exercises for students of varying abilities. Even better, once you've created it, you can go and have a coffee in the staffroom while Moodle grades it for you and gives your students an instant feedback, which they always appreciate!

For the purposes of this chapter, we're going to assume that the class has been learning about the major world rivers. So we shall:

♦ Test their knowledge with matching, gap-fill, crossword, multichoice, and jumbled up exercises that you don't have to mark

♦ Set a multimedia end-of-unit assessment test on Moodle that—once again—you don't have to mark

Forget the paper

In the past, we've been used to testing students' knowledge on paper and trying to find ways to make our worksheets a little more appealing than the usual question and answer format. I have spent many hours devising word searches and crosswords in MS Word—or making two columns with pairs of terms for my class to draw lines and to match up the correct pairs. You can do this, unless you want to kill time by getting the students to copy out all of the words in the columns, or draw the crosswords in their exercise books. However, the sheets are of no use once they've been written on. So forget the paper!

Hot potatoes—cool learning

Moodle can make quizzes and matching exercises as mentioned previously; with the added bonus that you don't have to mark them. We'll look at Moodle's offerings later in this chapter. However, there's another program available on the Internet that will enable you to do this kind of activity in double-quick time. It has a very bizarre name, which is, **Hot Potatoes**. It's not a part of Moodle, but it can be used in Moodle in a very simple and effective manner. Many teachers actually prefer it to the homegrown Moodle version. It has five types of activities that can be created while staying offline on your computer, and uploaded later to Moodle. What's more, you don't have to pay a single penny. So let's go and get it now!

 Hot Potatoes is free for download and use. It makes web pages which will give your students instant feedback on their scores. However, if you want to take it one step further, ask your Moodle admin to go to www.moodle.org and download the HotPot module. Then any scores your students get will be automatically recorded in Moodle's gradebook. Win-win for you and your classes!

Time for action – getting a program to create our self-marking activities

Let's download a program that will self-mark various activities. Hot Potatoes is one such famous program.

1. Go to the web address, `http://hotpot.uvic.ca/#downloads`.

2. For PC users, click on the **Downloads** link and then choose **Hot Potatoes 6.3 installer**. If you use Internet Explorer, you will get a message asking if you want to **Run or Save the Hotpot file**. If you use Firefox, you will be asked to **Save** it first, and Chrome will download it for you automatically. Once you have saved it, click **Run** to install it.

3. If you get any security warnings, agree to them and allow the setup to run (it's quite safe!). Click on **Next** to continue with the setup.

4. Select your language.

5. Accept the license agreement (as mentioned previously) and click on **Next** until the software has been installed.

6. When an image of a hand holding a potato appears, click on that image to bring up the following screen:

7. Click on **Help** and then click on **Register** (you first need to register—for free—to make full use of the exercises).

8. You're ready to go.

What just happened?

We have downloaded the Hot Potatoes program—which will enable us to make some self-marking exercises for our Moodle course—to our home computer. We had to register ourselves first to get started with the program, but that only took a moment and didn't involve any confidential details. Why not get your school technical support person to put it on your school's computers as well?

Each potato hides a different activity. We aren't bothered about **The Masher**. This helps you link Hot Potatoes together, but we don't need it. Once you've created a couple of activities, you'll get accustomed to the way they work, and you'll be creating them in no time at all. In fact, you can have a match up exercise created, uploaded, and ready for your students to use in less than ten minutes when you know how to do it. We're going to develop a lesson about famous rivers, on Moodle, using all five Hot Potatoes exercises. Here is a simple table that shows what they all do:

Name	What it does	Do we need it?
JMatch	Makes matching drag-and-drops	YES—it is simple and effective
JCross	Makes crosswords (including ones with images or sound)	YES—it has got a lot of potential
JCloze	Makes gap-fills of varying levels of difficulty	YES—It can be made as easy or as hard as you like
JQuiz	Makes multiple choice exercises	YES—It is simpler than the Moodle equivalent
JMix	Makes jumbled sentences	YES—It is a bit like magnetic fridge poetry
The Masher	Creates sequences of exercises that have been already made	NO—it's not really essential for us

Time for action – matching rivers to continents with the JMatch Hot Potato

I'm going to get my students to match up the five rivers with the continents they're situated in. I'm going to set a time limit on it: really quick—maybe a minute. Later, we'll do all of this together in lesson time, as I have a projector. I'll upload the exercise to Moodle so that for homework, they can each try to beat the time we got in class. Here it goes:

1. Click on **JMatch**. When the box comes up, type in a title and put your pairs in (correctly matched up) order, as shown in the following screenshot:

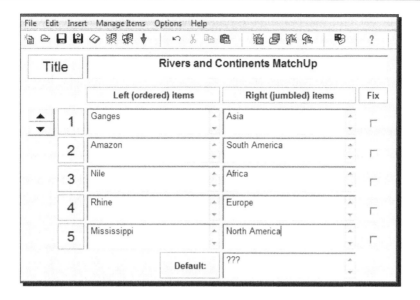

2. If you want more than five pairs, click the arrow next to **1**.

3. Once you have specified all of the pairs that you want to use, click on **File** and then click on **Save**. And you are done!

 That's as easy as it can be. However, you will get a rather blank and gray-looking matching exercise that will not inspire your students, visually, to give it a go. Let's try to pretty it up a bit first, before we save it and upload it into Moodle.

4. On the top menu bar, click on **Options | Configure output**, to display the screen as shown in the following screenshot:

5. Click on each tab and personalize your activity according to the following table:

Item	What it is	What I think
Title/Instructions	Change the default subtitle and instructions here.	Useful if you want to make the exercise simpler for younger students
Prompts/Feedback	Choose how you'll respond to right/wrong answers, and how you'll tell them their score.	Another way that you can personalize your activity
Buttons	More options to personalize the wording of the activity.	Important: Deselect the **next exercise** and **go to** buttons.
Appearance	Change the color of the page and text, here.	Click on the rainbow to select a color. This will be previewed on the screen, to the left. Do think of color-blind, dyslexic, and visually impaired students, though!
Timer	Set a time limit here and there will be a clock ticking away.	Select the **set a time limit** box; then you can choose seconds and/or minutes.
Other	Change the order of the items every time someone opens the activity here (if you want).	I never bother with this myself, but it helps if children are sitting next to each other and tempted to share answers.
Custom	Options for editing the code behind the activity.	Don't even look at this bit.
CGI	Lets people without Moodle send results via e-mail.	You don't need this!

6. When you are satisfied, click on **OK** at the bottom of the configuration screen to get back to your matching exercise.

 Let's have a quick look at **Buttons**. The Hot Potatoes program assumes that you're going to make a series of exercises. So, the Hot Potatoes program links them and automatically inserts a link on its page, which will lead you to the next exercise. However, as we are only going to be uploading one exercise at a time, we need to get rid of that link. Otherwise, the children—ever curious—will click on it and find that they reach a **Page Not Found** and may get confused. That's why it is important to deselect the two options mentioned in the preceding table.

7. Click on **File | Save as** to save the changes and give your matchup exercise a name.

What just happened?

We created and saved our first matching exercise using the Hot Potatoes **JMatch** option. We changed the color of the page, added a timer (30 seconds in this case), and abolished the confusing link buttons and non-existent exercises. We've now saved our exercise so we can adapt it any time we want, but to upload it to Moodle and to see how it looks we have to save it as a web page. To do that, we click on **File** and then on **Create Web Page**, as shown in the following screenshot:

JMatch has three different formats. I've listed and explained them in the following table:

Format	What it is	What I think
Flash card	Shows one pair; student guesses the match and then clicks to see if he or she is right	Useful for very young children to introduce/consolidate knowledge, but older students find it very boring
Standard	Gives one pair and a drop-down menu to choose the match from	Quite simple to see, but not very exciting
Drag/Drop	You drag the half on the right onto its matching pair on the left	Best for using with a projector and most popular with students too, especially when timed.

Have a go hero – make the rivers and continents into a drag-and-drop activity

Here's a small activity for you. Prepare a drag-and-drop activity for the rivers and continents.

1. Go to **File** and then click on **Create Web Page**.

2. Choose **Drag/drop** and save it, after giving it an appropriate name.

3. Choose the option **View the exercise in my browser**.

Try it!

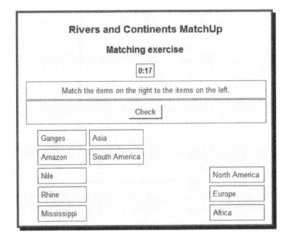

Students like colorful backgrounds added to their activities, but you have to be careful that you don't go over the top with gaudy combinations! The rivers and continents matchup is actually blue on yellow; one of the color schemes I understand is easily viewable by dyslexic children. You drag the continent (on the right-hand side) over to the river (on the left-hand side) to match them. Can you see the timer at the top of the screen? Once done, you need to click on **Check** to get your score.

Let's have a quick word about **Names**. Did you notice the first time we saved this activity by going to **File** and then clicking on **Save as**, its name (or filename) ended in .jmt? The second time it was saved, as a web page, it ended up in .html. If you want to alter the exercise, you need to make sure that you have the first version saved. It should be saved as it is in the project file, or else, the draft version might get edited. The other Hot Potato project files end in a similar way according to which one you are using— .jcl, .jcw, .jqz, and .jmx. To upload it to Moodle in the way we're going to do here, we need the .html file but if your admin installs the special HotPot module that will record all your students' scores for you, then it won't matter which one you upload—both will work fine on Moodle.

Okay, so we have created our matching activity. Remember that we had actually put the pairs in the correct order to start with? When it goes on Moodle for our class to do, it will get marked according to what we set up—so with that initial first effort, our marking is now at an end! Just one more step and that is, getting it up there for the children to try.

Time for action – getting our matching activity into Moodle

We have created the matching activity on our computer. It's now time to to upload it into Moodle.

1. With editing turned on, select **Add a Resource** and then select **File**.

2. In **Name**, type what you want your students to click on to get to the exercise and in **Description** explain what it's about. Check the box **Display description on course page** if you want this to appear on the main page:

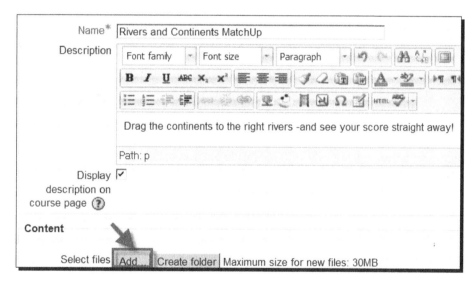

3. Click on the **Add** button to get to the **File picker**.

4. Browse your computer and upload the file, as we did for other resources and make sure you upload the `.htm` file.

5. In the **Display** options, choose **Automatic**.

6. Ignore all the other options for now (it's quite safe!).

7. Click on **Save and return to course**.

What just happened?

Our Hot Potatoes matching exercise is now in Moodle, and ready to be tried out! We uploaded it in a similar way we uploaded other resources such as Word-processed documents. The students will be able to do this exercise as often as they like and Moodle will show them their score. What it won't do, however, is show *you* their score. We'll take a look later at how we can make fun self-marking quizzes that keep the score for you as well as your students but before we do that, let's take a look at the other Hot Potatoes activities.

Want to get more out of Hot Potatoes?

Ask your Moodle admin to go to www.moodle.org and download the special Hot Potatoes module that keeps track of your students' scores. If you have that in your Moodle, you can upload your Hot Potato quizzes to a place in the **Add an activity** drop-down and you will be able to see results of every attempt your class has made.

Consolidating knowledge with Hot Potatoes activities

Once you've worked on one of the Hot Potato applications, you'll get the hang of the configuration screen and the process of uploading the exercise into Moodle. The other exercise types are fairly similar. It'd be quite nice to provide a selection for the students. However, in my experience, there's nothing wrong with using the same vocabulary or questions in each exercise. The students get to practice their learning in five different ways. Thus, by the end, they will identify with it—inside out and upside down! Let's re-jig our rivers and continents exercise in four new ways. The instructions don't need to be quite as detailed, now that we've got one under our belt.

Time for action – creating a self-marking gap-fill exercise

Let's re-equip the rivers and continents exercise and create a self-marking, gap-fill exercise.

1. Click on the **JCloze** Potato.

2. Give your gap-fill exercise a name by entering it in the **Title** box. In the window that pops up, type (or copy-and-paste) the passage in which you want to have gaps.

3. Select a word that you want blanked out, and click on **Gap** at the bottom of the screen.

4. If you wanted, you could add a clue and alternative correct answers for the gapped word, as shown in the following screenshot. If you aren't bothered about children's spelling, add alternative spellings, or if your word is a number, add it as digits here too:

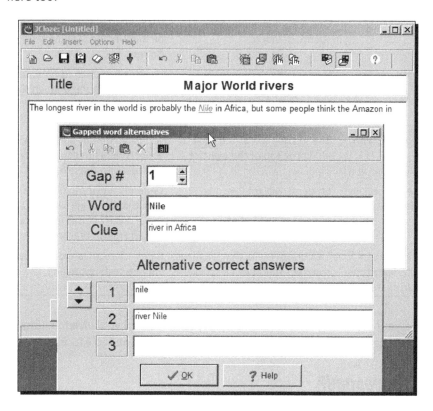

5. Click on **OK** to go back to the main screen.

6. Repeat this for as many blanks or gaps as you want.

7. Go to the configuration screen and personalize your exercise, as we did for the **JMatch** exercise.

8. Click on the **Other** tab, and, with the help of the following table, make your choices specific to **JCloze**:

Item	What it is	What I think
Include SCORM 1.2 functions	One way of including images, sound, or video.	We're not going to use this but I'll be mentioning SCORM in *Chapter 5, Games*.
Use a drop-down list instead of a textbox	Students don't type in their answers; they choose them from a list.	Use this if your children's literacy skills are not good enough that they can type in the answers by themselves.
Include word list with text	The missing words are shown along the top of the exercise.	You could do this and then get your students to copy and type the answers into the box.
Make answer checking case sensitive	Students will get it wrong if they use (for example) lowercase instead of uppercase.	Depends on whether you're testing punctuation or knowledge; I don't use it myself at this level—but I am not an English teacher.
Include a key pad to help the students type non-Roman characters	This brings up foreign language diacritics that they can click on to select them.	If it is a foreign language task and you are testing spelling, use it; if not—don't!

9. Save your gap-fill in a way similar to how you had saved your **JMatch**. Choose **Create Web Page** if you want to view and test it, and then upload to Moodle.

What just happened?

In double-quick time (I hope!) we used the **JCloze** Hot Potato to make a gap-fill, or cloze, exercise where our students have to fill in the correct rivers to go with the relevant continents. We have personalized its color and wording, perhaps added a timer, and are just about ready to upload it into Moodle.

Have a go hero – make differentiated exercises for students with mixed abilities

You must have noticed in the preceding table that the **Other** section provides you with two options to choose from. The first option will give a list of the missing words at the top of your gap-fill and the second option will offer a drop-down box for less confident spellers. Why not go and make two **JCloze** exercises? One **JCloze** exercise can be created for the students to have a guess and type in the names of the rivers or continents themselves with no help at all. Another **JCloze** exercise can be created where the students are provided with either the words to be copied by them, or a drop-down list. Alternatively, you could set a longer time limit for students with a lower ability, or allow them as much time as they need.

Time for action – making a self-marking crossword exercise

This one's probably my favorite. Don't be put off by it! As soon as you open it, it looks complex, but I have a method for creating the crosswords in double-quick time. Thus, let us just follow these instructions and then go and watch some TV. Crosswords are popular with some students, but not all children actually know how to fill them in. Also, the Hot Potatoes crosswords don't operate in the way you expect them to, so you might need to explain a bit about it to the students. Let's learn how to do it.

1. Click on **JCross**.

2. Type in the title of your crossword, in the box on the left.

3. Click on **Manage Grid**, which is available on the top menu and then click on **Automatic Grid Maker**.

4. Add the words that you want in your crossword, one under the other, as shown in the following screenshot:

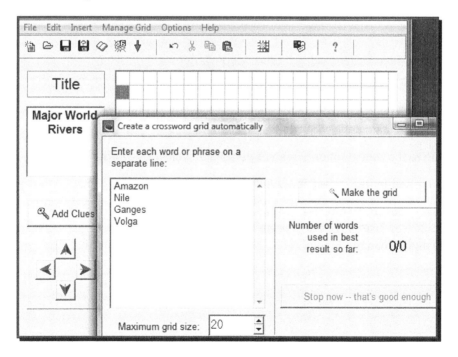

5. Click on the **Make the grid** button.

6. When you're happy with the results and are back on the main screen, click on **Add Clues**.

7. Select the word that you want to give a clue for. Type the clue in the box and click on **OK**, as shown in the following screenshot:

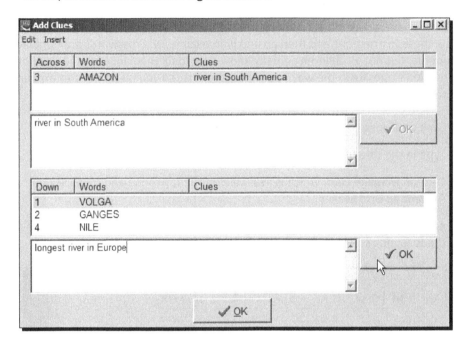

8. Click on the **OK** button—with the green tick mark—at the bottom of the screen, when you are done with adding the clues.

9. Go to the configuration screen to personalize your crossword.

10. In the **Other** tab, select **Show All** clues under the crossword grid.

11. Save your crossword, in a similar way, as you saved the **JMatch** and **JCloze** exercises. Use the option, **Create Web Page**, if you want to preview and test it and upload to Moodle.

What just happened?

We used the **JCross** Hot Potato application to create a crossword which our students can fill in online. They'll get their grades automatically and immediately. We have personalized the colors, made sure that the clues were listed under the crossword, and even set a timer. This exercise can be uploaded to Moodle in exactly the same way as the other Hot Potatoes applications.

Let's have a word about the crossword application. The Hot Potato crossword doesn't show the clues by default—that's the reason why, we made sure that we included them when we configured the display. Nor do you type your answers into the boxes—you type your answers by clicking on a clue number and then entering the word in the box that comes up. Try it—you'll need to explain this to your students before they attempt to solve a crossword.

Time for action – making a self-marking mixed up words exercise

Another application of Hot Potatoes is called **JMix**. This is helpful for creating activities where the students have to rearrange words or phrases. When you save it as a web page (`.htm`), you can set it up in two different ways. You can either set it up in such a way that when the students click on the word or the phrase, it magically moves itself into the next part of a sentence, or you can have it as a drag-and-drop activity. We're going to set up our application to put the correct rivers in the correct continents—again! This information will be indelibly printed on their brains once they've been through every Hot Potato! Let's learn how to set it up.

1. Click on **JMix**.

2. Enter a name in the **Title** box.

3. In the **Main sentence** box, type in your sentences—a few words at a time, separating them one under the other, as shown in the following screenshot:

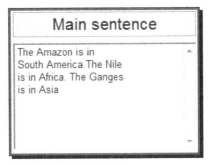

4. Think about possible alternative correct answers and add them to **Alternate Sentences**.

Alternate Sentences means that there is another way that the answer could be read, and still be right. For instance, if I did London/is/the capital of/ England, then it could work equally correct as the capital of England is London (if we disregard case). We need to enter that sentence as well, so that the children aren't penalized for a different turn of phrase.

5. Go to the configuration screen and personalize your exercise.

6. Save the exercise, in a similar way, as we saved the **JMatch**, the **JCross**, and the **JCloze** exercises.

7. Use the **Create Web Page** option to view this exercise in two different styles (standard or drag-and-drop).

What just happened?

We made use of the **JMix** application of Hot Potatoes, to create a scrambled up exercise where students will have to reorder parts of a sentence or sentences to make a meaningful passage. We shall upload it into Moodle in the same way as we loaded the other Hot Potatoes applications, although we have two ways of displaying it as an `.htm` file. Which one do you prefer?

The standard format appears as shown in the following screenshot:

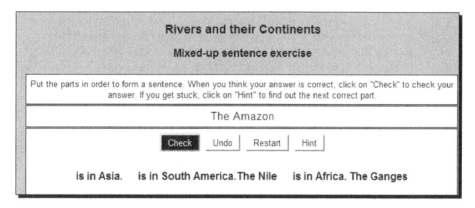

In the standard format, each time the students click on a word or phrase, it is attached to the previous phrase they clicked on. The drag-and-drop format looks like this:

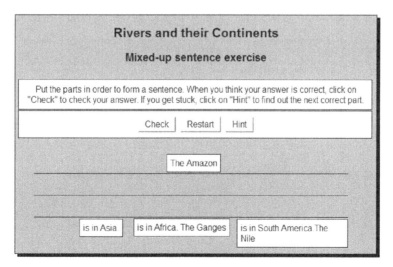

Your choice might depend on your personal experience with the students. Being a teacher, you'd know more about their preferences.

Time for action – making a self-marking multiple-choice quiz

There's a lot of "action" in this chapter! But it should get easier and quicker with each attempt. We're going to ask questions about rivers and the continents they're in, and give our students a choice of answers. You can make multiple choice quizzes in Moodle (and we shall), but Hot Potatoes are much simpler!

The first time that you click on the **JQuiz** potato, you'll be asked the question—**Beginner or Advanced**? This is to enquire whether you want to start in the beginner or in the advanced mode. The main difference between the two is that, with advanced mode, you can award percentages of marks to each alternative answer, unlike in the beginner mode—where only one answer is 100 percent correct, and the others are totally wrong.

1. Click on **JQuiz**.

2. In the **Title** box, enter a name for your exercise.

3. Type in your first question in the box next to **Q1**.

4. Type in the possible answers in the boxes next to **A**, **B**, **C**, and so on under the **Answers** heading.

5. If you wanted to, you could add **Feedback** for each answer.

6. Select the checkbox for the correct answer, below the **Settings** heading button.

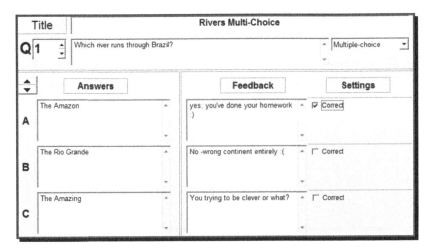

7. Click on the up arrow to the right of **Q1** to add another question.

8. Repeat the process until you're done adding all of your questions.

9. Go to the configuration screen to personalize your multi-choice exercise.

10. Save the exercise in the same way as you did for the other Hot Potatoes exercise, choosing **Create Web page** to preview and test your exercise, and then upload it to Moodle.

What just happened?

We used the **JQuiz** Potato to make a multiple-choice exercise to test our students' knowledge of rivers and continents. We have personalized the application's text and colors, and maybe added a timer, and are now ready to upload it into Moodle—just as we did the others.

 If you click on the drop-down menu and select the option **Multiple-choice**, (as shown in the top right corner of the preceding screenshot), you'll see that there are actually other types of question that we could have used.

Here's a table to explain what the drop-down menu options do, and why you might want to use them:

Type of question:	What it is	Why use it
Short answer	Students type an answer into a textbox.	Offers more scope, but you need to think of all possible permutations, or else, the students might find it tough to solve.
Hybrid	If they can't type in the correct answer after a certain number of tries, they get the question as a multiple-choice instead.	This might be useful if you think the students might have problems with your short answer questions. But if you think that way, why not just go for the multi-choice in the first place?
Multi-select	Students can choose more than one correct answer.	Useful if you want them to select a group of items—such as *Which of the following rivers are in Europe?*

How can we save the scores in Moodle

The way we've been making and uploading our Hot Potatoes activities, only our students can see their scores. If we want to know how well they did and if we want their scores to be recorded in Moodle's gradebook, we have three choices:

1. Instead of saving and uploading them as an `.htm` web page, we save them as SCORM package. I will show you how to upload SCORM packages in *Chapter 5, Games*.

2. We ask our Moodle admin to install the `HotPot` module which they can get from `www.moodle.org`.

3. We use Moodle's built-in quiz—which we'll look at next.

Words of warning

There is an important point to be made here—not to put you off Hot Potatoes, but just to make you aware.

Hot Potatoes quizzes are great fun and very useful as homework, consolidating what's been taught in class. However, they shouldn't really be used as assessment tests—crafty children, over the years, have found ways to get the answers without thinking too hard. They'll press the back button for instance, if they get one wrong, and allow themselves another try. Some of my students also have discovered that if you click on **Hint**, you get one letter of the word. When the **Hint** button is pressed again, you get another letter—until you get the whole word given to you. If you want to set a test in Moodle that you don't have to mark (and who wouldn't?) and is pretty much hack-proof, then you should use the Moodle quiz—as we shall be doing next.

Adding pictures, sound, or video to our self-marking exercises

So far, in this chapter, all our activities have involved words. Wouldn't it be good if we could spice them up a bit with sound, video, or pictures?

While it's possible to add multimedia like that to our Hot Potatoes quizzes, we're actually going to do this using Moodle's built-in quiz option as it's really easy to do. This will give us a chance both to take a look at how to make an activity in Moodle that gets marked for you, keeps the score for you and your classes, and is much more fun than just plain text!

Making an assessment test with a Moodle quiz

The name quiz is a bit of a misnomer really, as it makes me think of TV game shows. To Moodle, a quiz is just a module where you can add different types of questions for your students, which is not, usually, as exciting as it sounds (if you want excitement, read the next chapter on games!). What we're going to do is test our students' knowledge of the world's rivers in a timed assessment. Moodle's quiz isn't currently as friendly as Hot Potatoes, but I'm using it because it's safer for an exam.

Time for action – setting up a Moodle quiz as test on rivers and continents

Let's create a quiz to test our students' knowledge about the world's rivers in a timed assessment and let's jazz it up with some multimedia. From the **Add an activity** drop-down menu, we're going to choose **Quiz**. Now, it's over to you:

1. In the **Name** block, type a name for your quiz that the pupils will see and click on.

2. In the **Introduction** block, enter a description of the quiz. Check the box **Show description on the course page** if you want this to appear on the main page.

3. Select your options for the quiz in the boxes that follow—if in doubt, leave them the way they are; it's quite safe! Anything you don't understand, ignore!

4. Use the following table to help you make your choices (for our test, we need to set the timer as well as a password):

Item	What it is	What I think
Timing	Set start, end, and length of test—we've seen this before.	Select **Enable time limit** for them to see a clock as they work.
Attempts allowed	How many attempts they get, and if they will be penalized for extra attempts.	For tests, set it to **1** attempt. Set **Adaptive mode** to **No** and don't even bother to look at what it means.
Grading method	For a test, keep it at the highest grade.	Click the **?** icon to find out about the other options.
Grade	You can put this quiz into a category in Moodle's markbook	Ignore this if you don't understand it—the quiz will work fine.
Layout	How it will look on the page.	I'd choose **Shuffled** for **Question order** and **All Questions on one page**—but it's your call!

Item	What it is	What I think
Question behavior	Do you want questions at random and do you want students to answer them all before getting any grades?	Leave the settings as they are, but click on the **?** icon to find out about the other options.
Review options	When they get feedback and what feedback they get.	So many choices here—click the **?** for help, or leave it as it is.
Display	You can make Moodle show their picture as they do the test here.	Most of the time you can leave these settings as they are.
Extra restrictions	For setting a password and deciding how soon after they've done a test they can have another go.	Type in a password next to **Require password**—tell your class on the day. You can change it, for another class, another day.
Common module settings	For groups in the grade book.	Ignore unless your administrator has set you up with groups.
Overall feedback	Sets a comment at the end, according to how the students did.	A nice touch but you must fill in every box—see the following screenshot.

5. In the **Overall feedback** form, fill in your feedback—with respect to the marks the student scores. An example of how to begin this is shown in the following screenshot:

6. Click on **Save and display**.

7. You'll get the quiz front page—pointing out we have no questions yet—as shown in the following screenshot:

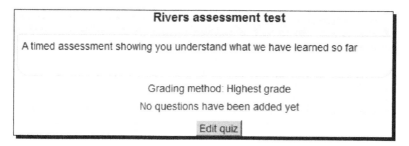

What just happened?

We've set up the front page of the Moodle quiz that will be our assessment test. We've decided on how the quiz will be presented to the students, and what feedback they will get. But, we haven't actually added any questions to it yet. In Moodle, we make an empty cover page first and then add questions to it. (See what I meant about Hot Potatoes quizzes being friendlier?)

Let's click on the **Edit quiz** button and get started. Here's what we then see:

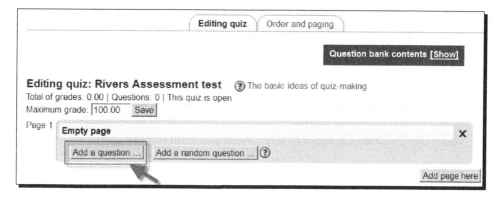

The quiz question screen

On the right are **Question bank contents**, the storage area for the questions. You can **Show** or **Hide** this. If you want to organize your quiz questions into categories, you can do that. However, we don't want any extra steps so, as beginners, we'll use the default.

To get started, we just click the button **Add a question** as in the screenshot. There are many different types of questions. However, some are easier when compared to others. Let's try the three easiest ones and then look briefly at the other possibilities later.

Time for action – making a multiple-choice question

Let's create a multiple-choice question in Moodle.

1. Click on **Add a question**.

2. Click on the button next to **Multiple choice** and then click on **Next** at the bottom.

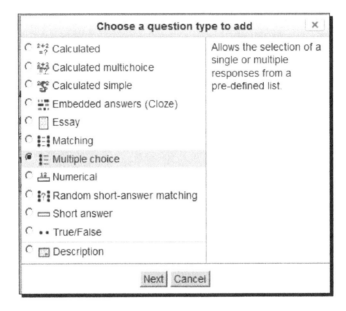

3. Leave the **Question Category** as it is (unless you want to change it).

4. In the **Question name** block, give the question a name—not *Question 1* (you put all of your questions for all your quizzes into here, so you need a more descriptive name for the question).

5. In the **Question text** block, type in the actual question.

Have a go hero – Jazz up the question with an image!

Remember we decided to try some multimedia in this test, because it is easy and will make the experience more fun for our students? You add pictures to quiz questions in the same way as you add pictures anywhere you see the image icon (the tree) in the text editor. So why not create a question where your class has to identify a part of a river by looking at a photo you've included?

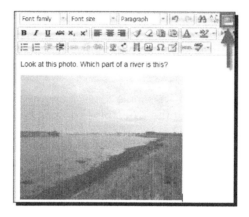

 Don't forget that you can make your textbox full screen by clicking on the top-right box as I have highlighted in the previous screenshot.

Ok, back to the question!

1. In the **Choice** sections, enter the alternative answers (with feedback, if you opted for it).

2. For the correct answer, change the **Grade** to **100%**, by selecting this from the drop-down menu. (Leave it at **None** for the wrong answers.)

3. Ignore all the other settings (though when you have more time you might like to investigate the **Hint** options) and click on **Save changes**.

What just happened?

We added our first question to our quiz front page! And we included an image. I uploaded one given to me by one of my pupils when she went on a family break. You could also find an image from Flickr that the author is happy to share with you because he has licensed it *Creative Commons*. An assessment with only one question is not much good. So let's move on.

Have a go hero – making a true/false question

If you can make one type of question, it's simple to make another. Why not practice including photos in your questions by trying out the **True/False** question type?

1. Click on **Add a question** and choose the option **True/False**.

2. Add your **Question name** and **Question text** as before, remembering to include a suitable picture.

3. I'll leave you to work the rest of the question out for yourself, but there is one thing that is really important to note. Make sure the **Correct answer True** or **False**, matches your statement as in my next screenshot; otherwise you will really confuse your children!

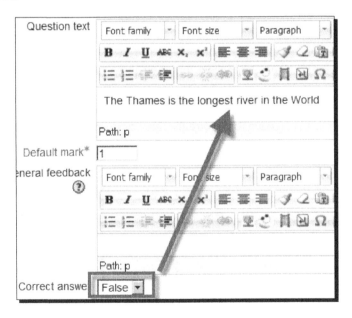

For the next question in our assessment test, we're going to add a video file. Our students will have to use their powers of observation to match up the beginnings and endings of the statements we're about to make.

Time for action – adding a video to a Matching question

Let's look at how to include a video file which our students much watch before they can answer the next question.

1. Click on **Add a question**; choose **Matching** and then click on **Next**.

2. For the **Question name** block, give your question a descriptive name (not number).

3. For **Question text**, explain that they have to watch the video and then match up the beginnings and endings of the sentences according to what they saw on the video.

4. In the text editor toolbar, click the filmstrip icon to upload a video of your own or to link to a video from YouTube, if it is allowed in your school. (We learned how to do this in *Chapter 3, Getting Interactive*, remember?)

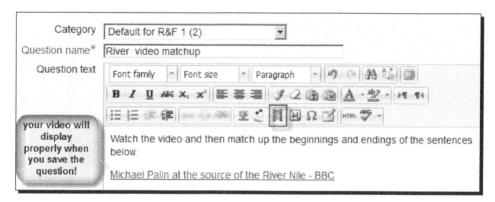

5. For each question, type a simple question in the **Question** box, and in the **Answer** field, type the answer. You need a minimum of three question/answer pairs for the matches to work. It doesn't have to be a proper question or answer. It can be the start and end of a sentence, as we are doing here:

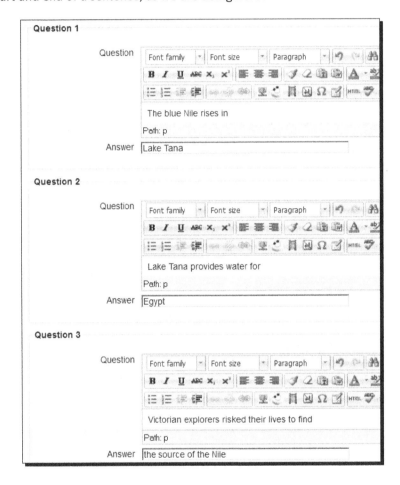

6. Click on **Save changes**.

What just happened?

We got even jazzier by adding a video to our question. Much more interesting than having our class read a lot of text, and of course, for students who find reading difficult, a visual question like this can be very motivating.

We put our video into a **Matching** question type, but you can add it to any question type. I find they work well in the **Multiple choice** question types.

Now that we know how to add video, it's not much different to add sound instead! Why would we want to do that?

- ◆ Our students aren't very good readers, but we still need to assess their knowledge
- ◆ We want to focus on improving the listening skills of our students

Have a go hero – Add a sound file to a quiz question

Remember when we click the filmstrip icon, a box comes up asking us to **Find or upload a sound, video or applet**?

If we have an .mp3 file on our computer, we can click that button to get to the **File picker** and upload our sound file into a question. The .mp3 file will play in its own little player like this:

If you have a .mp3 file already, why not make a multiple choice question that includes it?

Even better, why not check out *Chapter 6, Multimedia*, where we learn how to make our own .mp3 files as podcasts and add one of those that either you or a student made?

Previewing and using our Moodle assessment test

We've now got four questions in our quiz. The set up screen looks like this:

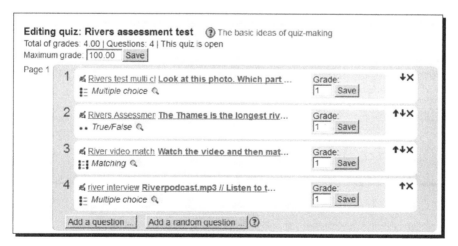

We can change how we grade each question in the grade box and we can re-order the questions by moving the arrows up or down. We can preview each question by clicking on the magnifying glass icon. Here is a preview of the video question, for example:

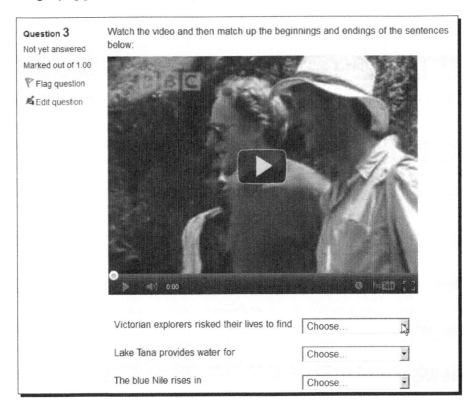

When the children click on the quiz link on the main course page, they can attempt our assessment. And how do we grade it? We don't. We just click the quiz link on the main course page ourselves when our students have done the assessment. Moodle will tell us how many students have attempted it and we'll be able to see precisely how long they took and which questions they got right or wrong—cool, isn't it?

First name / Surname	Started on	Completed	Time taken	Q. 1 /25.00	Q. 2 /25.00	Q. 3 /25.00	Q. 4 /25.00	Grade/ 100.00	Feedback
Chris LeNoir Review attempt	28 January 2012 09 30 PM	28 January 2012 09:30 PM	26 secs	25.00 ✓	25.00 ✓	8.33 ✓	25.00 ✓	83.33	Fantastic! You rule the rivers!

Other types of questions

For our assessment test, we have used the three simplest types of questions. At the start, I did say that there were other types of questions that are also a part of the Moodle quiz. The Moodle quiz is very powerful as it has a lot of potential and a variety of questions; but it is also very complex. I've summarized the other question types here. Some of them you might like to try. Others, I really wouldn't recommend, and would suggest that you look at Hot Potatoes instead:

Question type	What it is	What I think
Calculated	Numbers questions with formulae.	Perhaps more suited to older students.
Description	Not a question—just a space for some text.	You can use it as a passage on which you can base your subsequent questions.
Essay	Space for text and your question, and a student gets big space for long answer.	You have to mark this yourself— Moodle can't!
Short answer	The student types in a word or phrase, as his/her answer to your question.	You need to be careful to cover all possible permutations!
Numerical	For sums.	Looks like a short answer, but students type numbers instead of words.
Embedded answer or cloze	Moodle's version of gap-fill.	Needs some knowledge of coding; I find **JCloze** to be quicker to set up.

Summary

In this chapter, we've created a variety of activities to test our students' knowledge of the World's rivers. We've set up all the activities, which are going to mark themselves in Moodle. In this chapter, we created a matching exercise with words and a gap-fill exercise which can be adapted for both high-ability and low-ability children. We created a crossword that the students can enjoy solving, either individually on the computer or in the class using a projector. After that, we mixed up some clauses and got the students to think and reorder them correctly, and we then devised a multiple-choice exercise for homework. Finally, we designed a timed and password protected end of unit test in Moodle, with different types of questions.

I said at the start, that this chapter was all about work/life balance. After the work—of setting up my Hot Potatoes exercises and my end of unit assessment—I can now enjoy my life—sitting back and letting Moodle mark and record the grades for me. Next in *Chapter 5, Games*, it's time to play some games!

5
Games

This chapter is all about having fun! Not only do our students enjoy playing games that help them learn, but often, we enjoy watching them play—for everyone it acts as a welcome change from the dry textbook work. The following games are from sites that offer free or good value games for educational purposes. Games appeal to younger children because of their animations, sound effects, and (in a couple of cases) rather cruel nature! We're going to enhance our units on river processes and flooding by using some easy-to-set-up games. For one of the games, Moodle can do the grading for us—so while the students are enjoying playing, Moodle is keeping our gradebook updated.

In this chapter, we shall:

- Test our students' knowledge of flooding terminology with the help of a space-age hangman game

- Check the students' understanding of river processes with the help of a dustbin sorting game

- Make the students split mountains from rivers with the help of a great noisy hammer

- Test our students' memories with a Monster Memory game

- Assign the students homework—marked for us by Moodle—on the New Orleans flood. For this activity, their reward will be to catapult their Head Teacher (or us, the teachers!) into the sunset

So let's get on with it.

Making an Alien Abduction (hangman) game

The website that we're going to use for this game is `http://www.what2learn.com/`. This website has a number of free games that teachers can create online and link to from their Moodle site. I've found, as a High School teacher, that my 11-14 year old students are all too keen to look for game websites when they should be online working on their history homework. They'll actually love being able to play online games with your blessing—but you'll still have control.

Time for action – finding and making the Alien Abduction game

Let's first find and then create a game named **Alien Abduction**.

1. Go to the web address `http://www.what2learn.com/`.

2. Click on **Make game**.

3. Next, click on the link **Create a game** next to **Alien Abduction**. You'll see that there are other games as well—which you can create some other time.

4. Start typing in the names of the objects that you want to include in the game. We need to enter a title and eight words. Ours is about flooding; so it might look a bit like the following screenshot:

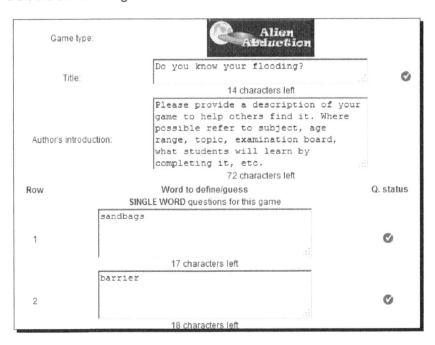

5. Check your words and click on **Create Game**. You'll then be asked to type in some letters to prove you are a human. Do that and click on **Submit**.

6. That's it! Done! You'll get the following message, displaying the number allotted to your game:

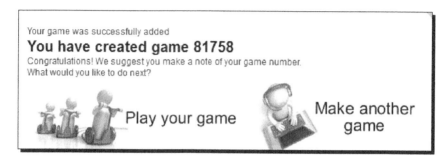

Your game was successfully added

You have created game 81758

Congratulations! We suggest you make a note of your game number.
What would you like to do next?

Play your game   Make another game

7. If you click on the link **Play your game** followed by the number allotted to the game, it will take you to your game, and you can play it right there. Copy the web address (URL) of this game. We'll need it in a moment.

What just happened?

We created a hangman-style game, online, by entering our choice of words and then saving the game on the website. We've been provided with a link to our game, which students can click on, to play the game.

In this game, children have to guess the words before the spaceship comes down and beams up Granny. Be warned—some of your students might deliberately get it wrong just to see what happens! It's only fair to let them do it once; I did, out of curiosity!

Have a go hero – adding a link to our game in Moodle

Now, we just need to get it into Moodle—which is something that we've already done several times in the previous chapter. Do you remember how?

1. With editing turned on, click on **Add a resource**.

2. Choose the option **URL**.

3. Type, or copy and paste, the link to the game into the **External URL** box.

4. Choose **Embed** for the display option.

5. Click on **Save and return to course**.

 A quick way to copy and paste a website address (URL) is to select it with your mouse and then press *Ctrl+C*, on the keyboard, and then go to where you want to paste it and press *Ctrl+V*.

Time for action – showing just the game without the web page

The way we've displayed our game also shows other parts of the web page that it comes from. What if you don't want your students to be distracted by all that? Is it not possible to display only the game and not the whole page?

Absolutely! Let's have a go; and in so doing, we'll learn a valuable skill for later on in *Chapter 7, Wonderful Web 2.0*.

1. Go back to the home page of www.what2learn.com and click on **Play game**.

2. Under option **One**, click the link **here** and then type in the game number.

3. Scroll right down to the very bottom of the screen where you will see the following screenshot:

Add this game to your blog, website or social networking page:

Link to this game:	http://www.what2learn.com/games/play/81758/
Embed (small):	<object classid="clsid:D27CDB6E-AE6D-11cf-96B8-44⸱
Embed (medium):	<object classid="clsid:D27CDB6E-AE6D-11cf-96B8-44⸱
Embed (large):	<object classid="clsid:D27CDB6E-AE6D-11cf-96B8-44⸱

4. Click inside the **Embed (medium)** box and copy (*Ctrl+C* on a PC) all the typing in there.

> You don't need to understand this to be able to do it! All that stuff is web code (HTML) which we are going to paste into a Moodle page to get the game to play immediately. (If you're concerned that the code might have a link back to the What2Learn website, get your techie admin to show you how to delete the link.)

5. With the editing turned on, click on **Add a resource | Page**, in the section you want your game to appear.

6. Give your page a name and description as we usually do.

7. In the **Page content** box, click the **HTML** icon before you do anything else.

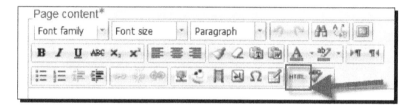

8. In the box that comes up, paste (*Ctrl+V* on a PC) the stuff you copied from the what2learn site.

9. Scroll down to the bottom and click on **Update**.

10. Save your page in the normal way as we've done before. When you return to the course and click on the page, you'll see the game—just the game—ready to be played without all the extra bits:

You might get a shock by the way: the sound effects come on as soon as you click on the page; so if you weren't expecting them, it will make you jump! You might want to tell your students that too—or perhaps not!

What just happened?

Instead of just linking to the page the game was on (which was easy) we found the webcode for the game and pasted that into a special code section of the text editor of a Moodle page. That's called **embedding** and it was more work, but meant that we just got the game and not the rest of the page. Embedding code from other websites is really useful, and you don't need to understand the code to be able to do it. In *Chapter 7, Wonderful Web 2.0*, we will take a look at other types of code we can embed to make our Moodle course more fun.

Garbage in the bins—making a sorting exercise

Our next game will get our students to separate the true statements about river processes from the ones that I have invented. The site I am using this time is `http://www.classtools.net`, a site made by teacher Russell Tarr for other teachers to use—for free. This website has a wide variety of activities that your students would love, but we're going to focus on the bin game. This needs one more step than our previous game did, but it is well worth that extra five minutes. Students enjoy playing the bin game, as they love the sounds made when they get the correct items in the correct bins.

Time for action – finding and making the bin game

Let's find and create a bin game, where the student is expected to decide which statements are true and which are false, by dropping the statements into the correct bin.

1. Go to the web address `http://www.classtools.net`.

2. Find **Templates** and then choose **Dustbin Game** as shown in the following screenshot:

- **Templates**
  - Fakebook
  - QR Game Generator [new!]
  - Arcade Game Generator
  - Random Name Picker
  - Countdown Timer
  - Twister
  - Keyword Checker
  - Plagiarizr
  - Dustbin Game
  - Telescopic Topic
  - Post It
  - Diamond 9
  - Fishbone (Ishikawa)
  - Venn Diagram

3. Click on the **Start** button under the garbage can!

4. Enter your statements in the text boxes (bins) available on the next screen. You'll have four bins; ignore the ones that you don't want to use. Change **category 1 name** to **True** and **category 2 name** to **False**:

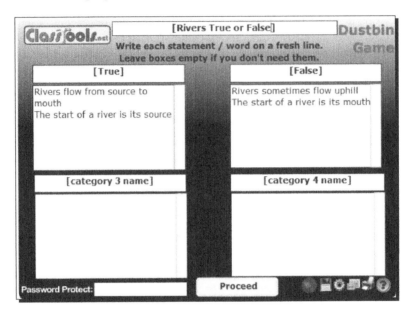

5. Enter a password in the **Password Protect** block, to stop students from being able to alter your words.

6. Click on the blue diskette icon, available to the right of the **Proceed** button.

7. When asked whether you want to open or save the file, choose to save it somewhere on your computer.

8. That's it. Done!

What just happened?

Earlier, we used another website (www.what2learn.com) to create a game that we access on that website. However, this time, we saved our game as a web page (an HTML file like those Hot Potatoes applications in *Chapter 4, Self-marking Quizzes*). When we go to Moodle, instead of linking to the website—where the game is—we actually upload that web page into Moodle.

Have a go hero (1) – adding a link to a file (our game) in Moodle

There's nothing tricky about this part. Upload the game file and the link to the game file in exactly the same way as you uploaded the individual Word-processed documents in *Chapter 2*, *Adding Worksheets and Resources*. (Choose **Add a resource | File**.) Then play it!

As each statement comes up on the screen, you need to drag the statement to the correct bin. Have your sound turned on. See what I meant about the children loving the noise?

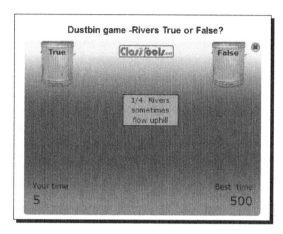

Have a go hero (2) – embedding the game into a Moodle page

We don't have to save and upload the `.html` file! Just as we did with the Alien Abduction game, we can get the code to paste or embed this game into a Moodle page.

1. Click the cogwheel icon to the right of the blue diskette.

2. It will open up a screen with embed code just like we had before. (You can even choose the size of the game on your page.)

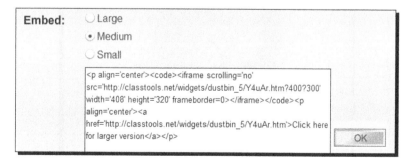

3. Now embed it into a Moodle page using the same instructions as for our Granny game before!

I've used this game in languages to get students to separate out masculine and feminine words. I have used the game in English to get the students to distinguish between nouns, verbs, and adjectives. In RE and PSHE, I've seen two bins—statements and opinions. The class must decide which sentences are true and which sentences are not.

Bish Bash Bosh—a differentiation game with a hammer!

The next game also requires the students to pick out words or concepts of a certain type from a group. But in this game, the students need speed and concentration. The aim of the game is to hit the correct words with a hammer, as they move along the screen. We'll get our younger students to separate mountains from rivers using **Bish Bash Bosh**—one of the several fun activities made by UK teacher, Stewart Davies. It's not like our first two games where you created the game online. We have to download the game making resources first. So, we have to put in slightly more effort, but it is well worth it. Let's take it one step at a time.

Time for action – finding and creating the Bish Bash Bosh game

Let's go online and then find the Bish Bash Bosh game.

1. Go to the web address `http://www.sandfields.co.uk/games/`.

2. Scroll down the page until you see the image shown in the following screenshot (which is what the game itself looks like):

3. Click on the **download link**, and a pop-up window will appear. Click on **Save**.

4. Navigate to the location on your computer where you saved the game. It should be a zipped folder (which has a zipper on its icon).

5. Right-click on this folder and choose **Extract All...** option:

6. Open the newly-extracted folder (which will have same name, but no zipper in the icon) and you should see the four files shown in the following screenshot:

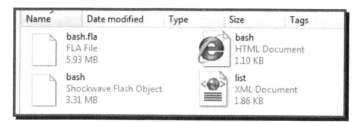

7. Right-click on the file called **list**, and choose **Open With | Notepad** from the context menu: (Mac users will choose **Text Edit**.)

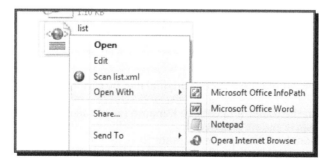

8. Don't panic! You'll see some French words placed in between a lot of punctuation marks (more web code, actually). They come in pairs: one word that's **right** (correct) and another one that's **wrong**:

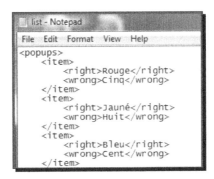

9. Enter the names of rivers (or names of anything, that you want to be selected) between the **right** tags.

10. Enter the names of mountains (or names of anything, that you want to be avoided) between the **wrong** tags:

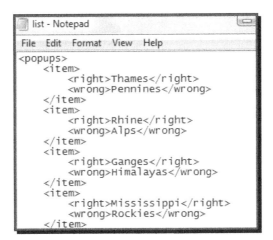

11. Overwrite this edited file with the original file, by clicking on **Save**.

12. Right-click on the folder and choose **Rename** (we'll call ours **Bashrivers**).

13. Congratulations! Another game is created!

What just happened?

We went to a website and downloaded a zipped folder containing a bashing, differentiation game. Once the folder was unzipped, we edited the file called `list.xml` to include the words that we wanted, and then saved it all again but with a new name. If you click on the `.html` file in that new folder, you can actually play the game on your computer. It's hard—you have to chase the river names and bash them with a hammer (great sound effects again), and at the same time you have to avoid the mountains.

Now, it's time to get our game into Moodle.

Time for action – uploading and displaying our game on Moodle

As you may recall, Moodle won't let you upload folders in the way that they are normally stored on your PC. You have to zip or compress them first. Then, once you have uploaded them into Moodle, you have to unzip them again and select the main file to play the game.

1. Right-click on our game folder and choose **Send To | Compressed (zipped) Folder**:

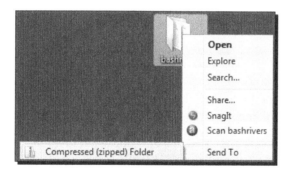

2. From your Moodle course page, with the editing turned on and in the section you want the game to be, click on **Add a resource | File**, and then upload this zipped folder (the file should have an extension of `.zip`).

Make sure you choose **File** and not **Folder**. Odd though it seems, we aren't uploading our folder to the **Folder** section. We have to add it to the **File** section because all our game files are linked together. You *can* add folders to the **File** option in Moodle.

3. Once the file has been uploaded, click the little icon to the right of the zipped folder and then choose **Unzip**.

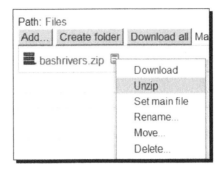

4. You'll then get the folder again but in its normal shape: (You can click the icon next to the zipped one to delete it if you want to, but you don't have to.)

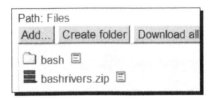

5. Click the name of the unzipped folder to open up its contents. You'll see the files that we edited offline.

6. Click the icon next to the **.html** file and choose **Set main file**:

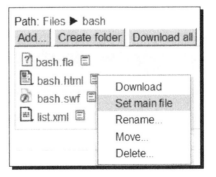

7. It will now appear bold. This is going well.

8. Choose your preferred display and other settings.

9. Click on **Save and return to course**.

What just happened?

We downloaded a folder of files to create a game offline that we then upload to Moodle as a zipped folder using the **File** resource. We unzipped it, set the `.html` file as our main file to display and we now have our students practicing their rivers by bashing them with a hammer!

 Did you notice that the file we altered ended in `.xml`? This is like an information sheet that passes the details onto the rest of the game to make it work. Once you understand that, there are several games that work in the same way—you're about to create another one now.

Have a go hero – make a wheel of fortune game

The site we got our Bash Hammer game from, `www.sandfields.co.uk`, is packed with free fun games involving these `.xml` files. Why not go back there and download the **Flip-Flap** game which is a bit like **Hangman** or **Wheel of Fortune** and see if you can adapt and upload a version of that to your Moodle course?

Making a Monster memory game from Languages Online

Our next game also makes use of XML files but it keeps them easy for us as we can just edit the words from inside the game, rather than editing the XML file directly. **Languages Online** is an Australian educational website (`http://www.eduweb.vic.gov.au/languagesonline/`) which provides free downloadable game makers that are particularly suited to language learning. Unfortunately, at the moment they only work on Windows computers, but as many schools use Windows we're going to give it a try. We're only going to look at Memory Game Maker, but if you investigate the site, you'll see you can also create Tetris games, Matching games, or even generate your own cartoon stories. And, there are some readymade games to get you started.

Our game is like **Concentration** or **Pelmanism**, where you are given a set of cards, face down, and you have to match up pairs of cards by remembering where they are in the set. Our game has windows of a castle that our students click on to find matching rivers and cities. If they get it right, the monster waves the flag. If they get it wrong, they get a negative sound effect—of our choice!

Here's what the finished game looks like:

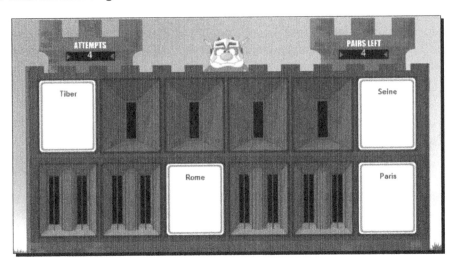

Time for action – downloading Memory Game Maker

First we need to download Memory Game Maker so we can start work on it. Let's do that now:

1. Go to http://www.eduweb.vic.gov.au/languagesonline/.

2. Click on the **Memory Game Maker** link as in the following screenshot:

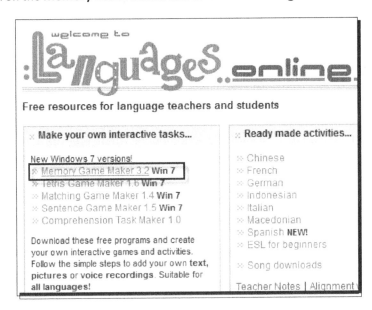

3. Click on **Memory Game Maker** in the next link:

4. When prompted to run or save, click on **Save**. (If you use Firefox as your web browser, you will only get the **Save** option.)

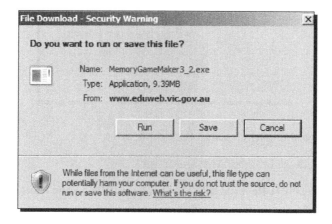

5. When the game maker has downloaded, click to open it. If you get any security notices, say **Yes**. It is quite safe.

6. Follow the instructions for it to install itself, clicking on **Next** when needed.

7. Now click the **Game Maker** icon to open it; click **Create new game** and let's get started!

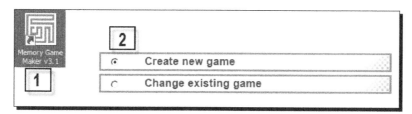

What just happened?

We've downloaded one of the games offered us by the Australian site Languages Online. We saved it to our computer and clicked the icon to open it and created a new game.

Time for action – creating our memory game

To create our memory game, we click through a number of stages by clicking on **Next step** at the bottom right of the screen.

1. Give the game a title and add your name.

2. Choose how many pairs of cards you wish to use. (We'll choose **6**.)

3. Choose the design of the game. We're choosing the Monster **Castle** game:

4. Choose a sound to play for when they get it wrong.

5. Choose a message for when they get it right.

6. Choose **TEXT**, **PICTURE**, or **SOUND** for each row. We'll keep it simple with **TEXT** for both rows.

7. Type in words that match top and bottom, as in the next screenshot:

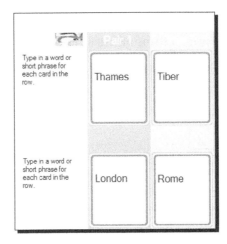

8. Save the game as a `.zip` file:

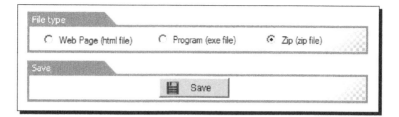

What just happened?

We went to the Australian site Languages Online and downloaded one of their Game Maker programs which are templates for different types of vocabulary games. We made a memory game and saved it as a ZIP file. Now it's over to you!

Have a go hero (1) – upload the game to Moodle

The file we saved is a zipped (compressed) file and it needs to be uploaded to Moodle from the **Add a resource | File** option. Once the file is uploaded, it must be unzipped. The `.html` file must be set as the main file. Sound familiar? We did exactly this with the Bish Bash Bosh game. So give it a go now.

Have a go hero (2) – create a different type of game

And now you've got the hang of how these games work, why not go back to `http://www. eduweb.vic.gov.au/languagesonline/` and download a different vocabulary game maker to see how popular that one might be?

I know what you're thinking!

We're having a lot of fun creating games. We've made two types of online games and two types of offline games that we've uploaded onto Moodle. Our students will have a lot of fun playing these games, and will appreciate the instant feedback that the activity offers. However, how do we get this past the Head Teacher or parents who see no evidence of what the students have actually achieved? Well, how about making a game that actually records their scores in Moodle?

Fling the Teacher—making a Moodle-marked homework

Fling the Teacher is yet another free game created by yet another teacher, Andrew Field (Where do these teachers find the time?). Its advantage is that it links to the gradebook in Moodle in a way that is not so different from the Quiz which we worked on in the previous chapter. So, while our youngsters think they're playing a game for homework, you get their results saved in Moodle, to justify their fun!

What's more; I've saved the best until last! In Alien Abduction—our first game—the idea was to save granny from being zapped by the aliens. The idea here is that our pupils' knowledge won't save their teacher; rather, it will condemn the teacher! It's much more motivating that way! As each question is answered correctly, a trebuchet is constructed, with the head of their teacher on it. Eventually, if all of the questions are answered correctly, the teacher is flung. There is an option at the start to customize the teacher's appearance. I'm not saying that the drawn face will exactly look like that of our Head Teacher. However, I have seen many games played on Moodle with a balding, bespectacled man!

Let's make a game for our eighth year class students (12-13 year olds), who've been studying the flooding in New Orleans that happened after Hurricane Katrina struck. We watched a documentary about the hurricane in our class, and for homework, they were asked to demonstrate how much they could still recall by playing the game, Fling the Teacher.

Time for action – finding and setting up Fling the Teacher

Let's set up the game, Fling the Teacher.

1. Go to the website address `http://www.contentgenerator.net/`.

2. Scroll down and click on the **Free** link, available under the **Fling the Teacher** image.

3. Scroll down to **Suite 2**: **Fling the Teacher**, and click on the title.

4. Scroll down to the bottom of the screen and click on the **Download File** link.

5. A dialog box will be displayed, as shown in the following screenshot. Check the **Open with** radio button and then click **OK**.

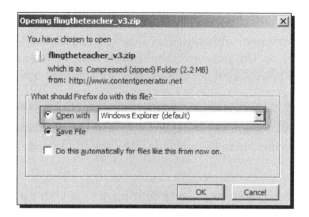

6. When it has opened, click on the **Extract all files** button and let the program install itself. Click **Setup** for it to set itself up on your computer.

7. You might be asked if you want to allow this or not. Choose to allow it.

8. Keep clicking **Next** until you get to the end of the install.

9. When the installation has finished, the game should open up on your computer, and you will get this screen:

10. Click on the icon with the star, located to the left of the screen. (The tooltip text will say **Create a New Game**.)

What just happened?

We just downloaded, unzipped, and opened up another free program that we will use to create a self-marking game. This game will then be uploaded into Moodle and have its scores recorded in the gradebook. Let's get back into action straight away, and create the game!

Time for action – creating a Fling the Teacher game

Now, that we have searched for and downloaded the Fling the Teacher game, let's go ahead and create the game.

1. On the first screen that is displayed when you click on **Create a New Game**, type the title of your new game and your own name (if you want).

2. Click on **Continue**.

3. Type in your question in the **Question** box, as shown in the following screenshot:

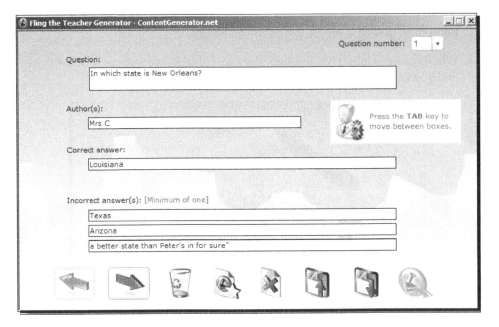

4. Click on the right-pointing arrow at the bottom of the screen to continue.

Did you see the final incorrect answer that I have entered? We're creating this game for one particular class, and they'll love it if we can personalize it a little—by making references to students in the group or even teachers in the school. I discovered, several years ago, that children are more motivated to persevere with an activity if they think there's a chance they might feature in it somewhere! Keep that in mind as you do the games in this chapter.

5. After a minimum of 15 questions, the icon to the far right will become clickable. If you hover your cursor over it, it says **Game set up**. Click on it now! The screen will appear as in the following screenshot:

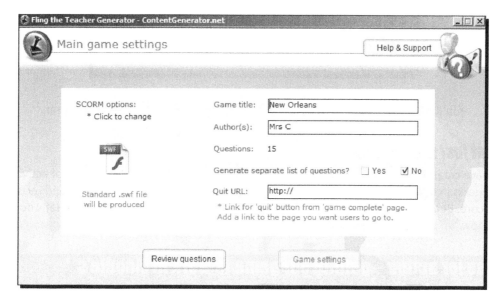

6. We want the SCORM option because this will work with our Moodle gradebook so we click ***Click to change** and we will see the words **SCORM compliant zip file will be produced**.

7. Click once more on the **Generate game** icon on the far right. You will be prompted for a location to save the game file to, as shown in the following screenshot:

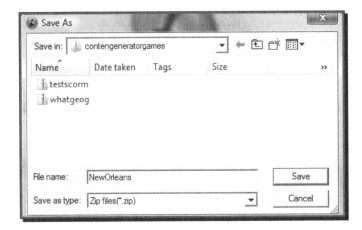

8. You'll be saving the game as a compressed (zipped) folder on your computer.

What just happened?

We have created our game and saved it in a SCORM activity. This is a special type of activity that works in different **Virtual Learning Environments (VLEs)**—such as Moodle—and records the score. Because of this, we need to upload it in a special way for it to work. So, let's do that now:

Time for action – getting our game to work in Moodle's gradebook

Now that we have created the game and downloaded it to our computer, let's get the game uploaded into Moodle.

1. With editing turned on, click on the **Add an activity...** option.

2. Choose the option **SCORM package**

3. You'll get a screen with the options that we've never come across before. Don't panic!

4. The **General** settings are the same as for other activities.

5. For **Type**, choose **Uploaded package**.

6. Click **Choose a file** and upload your zipped folder (**NewOrleans.zip**) as in the following screenshot:

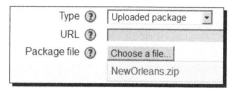

7. Don't worry that you can't unzip it. You don't need to.

8. Set your options to be the same as the ones shown in the following, rather long, screenshot. (If you're missing some options, click on **Show Advanced** to reveal them.)

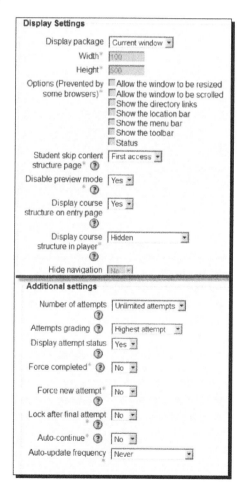

SCORM types of activity, like this one, need several files to work, and are quite complex. Fortunately, we don't need to understand any of those files to get them onto our Moodle site. Just ensure that your settings are the same as mine, and your teacher will get flung into your gradebook—no problem.

Have a go hero – playing the game

Now that you've completed the complex part, you get to do the fun part—checking if everything works by playing the game! If you go back to the course page, you'll see that our game has its own icon next to it—a bit like a box—which indicates that it is a SCORM activity (for those who really want to know). Click on this icon to play the game. When you get the first question and choices of answer, you'll notice that you also have three lives, unlike the other games we have created.

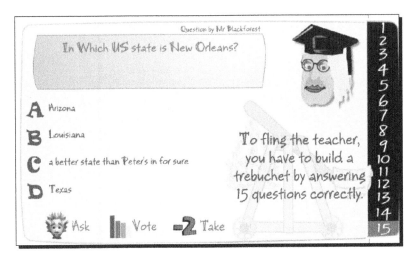

You have to get all 15 questions correct in order to build the trebuchet and fling the teacher. As soon as you get one answer wrong, the game stops. You'd be amazed (or maybe not!) at how many students will play the game again and again until they get all of the questions correct, in order to do the dirty deed. Eventually, while the students think that they're just playing, we know that by repeatedly checking the answers, they are memorizing the facts!

Once the game is over, you can check the students' scores by clicking on the **Grades** option—which is available in the **Settings** block in the **Course Administration** area. You will see the results displayed as shown in the following screenshot:

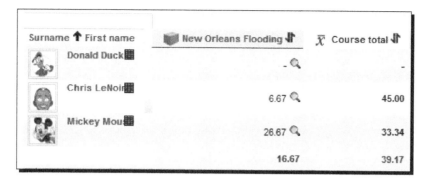

Surname ↑ First name	🎁 New Orleans Flooding ⇕	𝑥̄ Course total ⇕
Donald Duck▦	- 🔍	-
Chris LeNoir▦	6.67 🔍	45.00
Mickey Mou▦	26.67 🔍	33.34
	16.67	39.17

There are more games, like Fling the Teacher, available on the Internet. Fling the Teacher is a free game for all teachers to use. If you like it, you can find similar free games, plus some good value paid-for games, on the website http://www.contentgenerator.net/. You can play soccer, have a swordfight, play Teacher Invaders, and more. Now that you know how to make the games work in Moodle's gradebook, you'll have no problem with adding extra activities.

Summary

In this chapter, we've consolidated pupils' knowledge of our rivers and flooding topics by creating five free games for the students to enjoy. We have created two games, entirely online, and linked them into our Moodle course page by using the **URL**, **Page**, or **File** option. After that, we made two other games, which we downloaded and, by changing a special (.xml) file, we customized for our purposes. We then uploaded a zipped folder containing the required files into Moodle and linked to the .html file that displays our game. Finally, we generated a fifth game, which we downloaded, added questions to, and then uploaded in a special way (SCORM) that ensures that the results are saved in Moodle.

So far, so good! In this chapter and the previous one, we have used other people's creativity for our own teaching purposes. But what about being creative ourselves? And what about bringing out the creativity of our own students? In the next chapter, we shall do just that, using Moodle as our showcase.

6
Multimedia

This chapter is all about sound and vision. A big plus for teachers using Moodle is that we're not just tied to displaying worksheets that we've had for years. Our classes can watch movies, listen to interviews or stories, and even make their own audio visuals for other students to enjoy. As part of our Rivers and Flooding project, we're going to get our students involved in producing content for Moodle and we're also going to be creative ourselves.

In this chapter, we shall:

- ◆ Make a sound recording of one of our students reading a rivers poem
- ◆ Make a short film about a field trip our class went on, using students' photos and a narrative read by another member of the class
- ◆ Upload the recording and the short film into Moodle to show the students' parents how talented they are

The term **multimedia** is applied to many ways of communication. People learn in different ways: some prefer to listen, some prefer to read, and some prefer to watch and learn. We try in our classroom to cater to different learning styles by adapting our teaching methods to suit both Jane, who is a visual learner and Johnny, who is a kinesthetic learner. So if we can use different ways to communicate our subjects, we are more likely to hit the target with our pupils. Within Moodle, we can use multimedia to give variety to the tasks that we set. In this chapter, we're going to use the media of sound and video.

Making a sound recording to put into Moodle

Perhaps you have an iPod or an MP3 player. Maybe you download music or talk shows. The files you listen to, or download, are similar to what we are going to create for Moodle. Some people call them podcasts. Although our creations are not podcasts in the strictest terms, we're pretty close!

How do we do it? Well, we need a script to be read out. For that, we shall use a poem written by Jamie, a ten year old student in my class. All we need now is the equipment and an instrument to record him with. We need two, or possibly three, items:

1. A computer.
2. A microphone, if your computer doesn't have one built-in.
3. A free program called **Audacity**, which we'll download in a moment.

You don't need an expensive broadcasting-standard furry microphone at all; a basic mike that gets plugged into your computer will do the job for us.

You should find a socket with an icon of a mike somewhere at the back or sides of your computer or laptop that you can plug the microphone into.

Time for action – getting Audacity

We need a software program for recording sounds. Let's download the software program Audacity. It is a free open source program for recording and editing sounds.

If you already have Audacity installed (some teachers might have it installed on their school computers), then you can skip the first two steps.

1. Go to the website http://audacity.sourceforge.net/.

2. If you are running Windows, click on the **Download Audacity** link. This will have numbers next to it for the latest version; at the time of writing (March 2012) this was version 2.0. If you have a Mac, click on **Other downloads**.

3. Follow the instructions on the next screen; the download will start automatically.

4. When the download has finished, go back to the website, http://audacity. sourceforge.net/download/windows.

5. Click on the **Lame MP3 encoder** link, and follow the instructions on the next screen.

What is the Lame MP3 encoder? The best format of the sound file for us to put into Moodle is an MP3 file—the format of songs you might like to listen to and download. In order for Audacity to save our recordings in MP3 format, we need to download this oddly-named piece of kit. A nuisance, but we only need to do it once!

The Audacity logo looks as shown in this screenshot.

I have mine as a shortcut on my desktop. What we need now, is our microphone (if we don't have an inbuilt one), a quiet place to record (if there is such a place in your school!), and our voice—Jamie—and we are ready to go!

What just happened?

We just downloaded a free program that allows us to record audio directly onto our computer. We also downloaded an add-on that will enable us to save our recordings as MP3 files—the most popular format to put on Moodle. We clicked on the files ending in .exe to install them on our computer.

Time for action – setting up to record

We have downloaded the software application named Audacity for the purpose of recording audio. Now, let's set up the Audacity application.

1. Click on the Audacity logo. Don't worry about the complex-looking screen; we only need to use a couple of the features.

2. Make sure your computer's sound is switched on. Check the loudspeaker icon on the bottom-right corner of your screen. If it has a red **X**, it's off. Click on that icon to turn the loudspeaker on.

3. Click on the red recording circle and speak out loud. If you are able to see sound waves on the screen, as shown in the following screenshot, you have an inbuilt microphone. Click the square button to stop. You can move on to step 8.

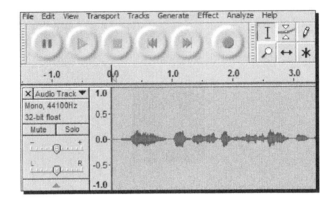

4. If you don't have an inbuilt microphone, you'll need to connect an external microphone. If you have an external microphone, plug it into the computer now, making sure that it's turned on.

5. Go to menu option **Edit | Preferences | Devices | Recording** and select the name of your microphone from the drop-down menu:

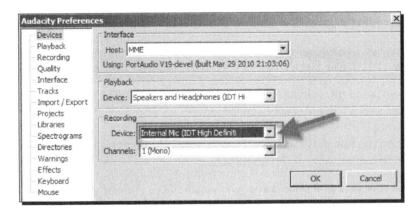

6. Click on **OK**.

7. Next, click on the red record button. Speak, and check whether you get the sound waves this time.

8. Look at the size of the sound waves when you pressed the red button to record. They need to be in the range of **0.5** and **0**. If the range is anywhere above or below this range, your sound will be too loud or too quiet.

What just happened?

We have tried recording our voice using Audacity, either with an inbuilt microphone or with the one we have attached to our computer. We checked whether the sound was at the right level and now we're ready to move on.

Have a go hero – recording audio

It's over to you now! If you've still got Audacity open, which we used for our trial run, then go to the top-left corner of your window; click on the **X** button to the left of the **Audio Track**, as shown in the following screenshot. Clicking on the **X** button will clear your screen. Now, be ready to record yourself, or in our case, Jamie!

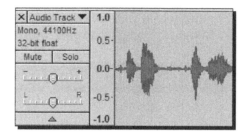

Check that Jamie is neither too near nor too far from the microphone. Click on the red record button to start recording. Click on the square stop button to stop. You can pause to gather breath by clicking on the pause button—available on the far left, as shown in the following screenshot. (The buttons are similar to the buttons on DVD or video players—aren't they?)

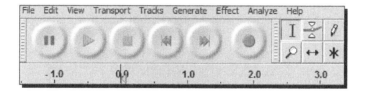

Improving the recording and involving our class

If we're happy with the recording, once we've pressed the stop button, we can save it and that's about it. But sometimes, it isn't that simple. In this section, we'll have a very quick look at how we can improve our sound file.

Audacity gives us lots of options for all types of fancy sound effects. We can disguise our voice by speeding up or slowing down the recording. We can also add an echo effect, sound effect, or background music to the recorded voice. The creative possibilities of Audacity would make up a book on their own. (Indeed, Packt has published one!) We cannot do them justice in just one part of our chapter. If you ever have time to play with the other controls, do so—the fun results would be worth it!

But if you can't set aside the time, why not make Audacity a class project for your students to perform, and upload their productions into the Moodle? We recorded one student, just to become familiar with the program. Why not now pass the buck onto the rest of the class and get them to record their poems themselves? The youngest students I have practiced this method on have been nine years old. However, I firmly believe that with careful instructions, children younger than this could succeed, too. The main advantage that the students have over us is that they will not be afraid to play with the other controls. Eventually, the students could well produce podcasts of a higher standard than ours, with more imaginative effects.

Time for action – getting rid of the coughs and giggles

Let's just look at a few ways to enhance our effort. After that, we'll put the audio recording into Moodle.

1. Play the audio that you have recorded by clicking on the green play button.

2. Find the part of the recording with the cough, giggle, or any other error that you want to cut out from the recording.

3. Use your mouse to select that bit of the file, just as you would highlight a word when typing. In the following screenshot, you'll find that the chosen section is darker:

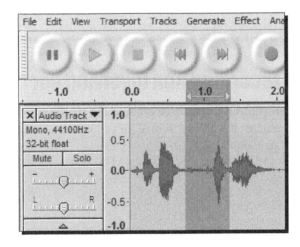

4. Press the *Delete* button on your keyboard, or click on the scissor icon on the Audacity toolbar. Done!

What just happened?

We learned how to cut out bits of our recording, that we didn't want, by selecting them and then deleting them.

Time for action – adding background music

Now that we have removed all of the imperfections in our recording, let's make it a bit more interesting by adding some background music.

> Although it's tempting to rip our students' chart-topping favorites off a CD and add them to our podcast, copyright rules just don't allow us to do this. We can have up to 30 seconds of professional music, but if our track is long, it's safer (and nicer for our students) to record and use music they've made themselves. Alternatively, we can go to the Creative Commons website, `http://creativecommons.org`, and search for a suitable music track there.

Let's assume that for Jamie's poem we have a music file that one of the music classes have already made for us. It should end in `.mp3` or `.wav`. What next?

1. Select menu option **File | Import | Audio**:

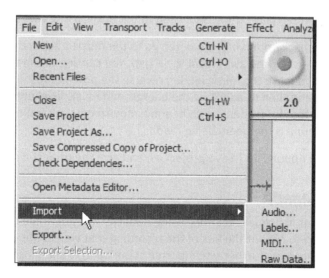

2. Browse for the music file that you want to be played.

3. Select it, and click on **Open**.

4. The file will appear underneath the track that we've just selected.(Don't worry if there are two extra tracks.)

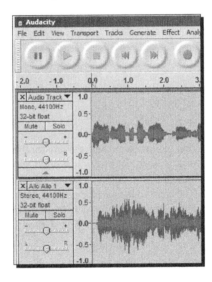

5. Shorten the music file length, if necessary, by using the cough or giggle deletion method.

6. Click on the green play button and listen to the music along with the voice.

7. To make the background music quieter, go to the music track and move the slider towards the – sign, and away from the + sign. You can see this in the previous screenshot. To make the music louder, reverse the process. Test it by clicking on the play button and then re-adjusting the background music level until you are satisfied. (Remember that for students with hearing impairments, it's important that the dominant sound is the poem being read.)

8. Select menu option **File | Save project as**, and give the project a name.

What just happened?

We've just created our first voice recording using Audacity. We got Jamie to record his poem, which we then edited to cut out the bits of the recording that we did not want. Then, to improve the audio recording further, we imported some background music, made it fit the length of the poem, and reduced the volume of the imported music so that it didn't drown out Jamie's voice. We then saved the entire recording as a project file.

This means that, if we want to go back and improve the audio recording another time (change the music and add some effects) we can open the recording up again and edit it. But, if we're going to have a finished podcast ready for Moodle, we should export it (the term Audacity uses) as an MP3 file. The first time that we do this we'll get a message asking us to locate the Lame MP3 encoder that we downloaded at the beginning of this chapter. Hopefully, you can remember where you downloaded the file to and are able to select it. From then on, the procedure will be the same each time that we create our masterpiece and we won't need to worry about this Lame MP3 encoder.

Time for action – saving our recording

We have created the audio recording with the help of Audacity. Now, we need to upload it into our Moodle course. We first have to save it on our computer.

1. Go to **File | Export** and make sure the drop-down is showing MP3.

2. You'll be directed to your hard disk drive. Find a place to save your file on the hard disk, and give it a name.

3. If you get a message saying that the computer is saving your tracks into one single track, just agree!

4. When the box (shown in the following screenshot) appears, add the required information about the file, and then click on the **OK** button:

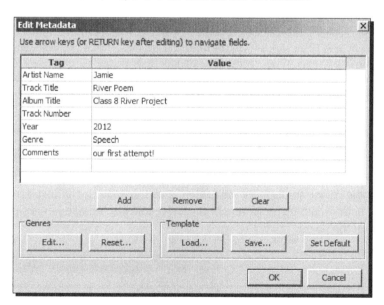

What just happened?

We did it! We have created and saved our sound recording! We saved it as an MP3 file, the best type of sound file for Moodle. More importantly, we now have the skills to show the students how to make their own recording. Why not play the file now and see how it sounds? Then, we'll look at two ways of playing it into Moodle.

Have a go hero – displaying our MP3 file on Moodle

Let's upload the audio recording file, which we have saved on our computer, into our Moodle course.

1. With editing turned on, select menu option **Add a resource | File**.
2. Click the **Add** button, as we've done many times before.
3. From the **File picker**, click **Upload a file**.
4. Browse for and choose the poem recorded by Jamie.
5. Click on **Save and return to course**.

Hopefully, you will have noticed that what seemed like a very tedious affair the first time we uploaded our creation into Moodle has now become much less of an effort through practice.

If you're satisfied with displaying Jamie's poem in the way you have, stop here and have a coffee. It's fine! If you want to be a bit smarter, read on.

 You can play the MP3 files, and the movies we're about to create, in their own neat little players—like the ones you see on YouTube and other websites. However, your admin needs to have Moodle set up for this purpose—check with them first. Ask them whether the multimedia plugin filters are enabled for .mp3 and .wmv. If they say yes, you can do the next bit!

Time for action – displaying the audio file in a player on the page

Want your Moodle course to display your audio file as shown in the following screenshot? Follow the instructions under the screenshot! Let's see how to upload Jamie's podcast so it displays nicely on the page:

Jamie's river poem - with music!

1. Click on the **Turn editing on** button.

2. Under **Add a resource**, select **Label**.

3. Type in some words to introduce the MP3 file and then click the Moodle media (film strip) icon:

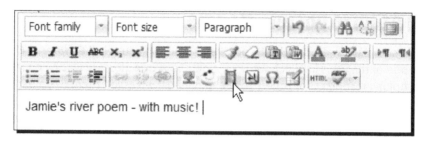

4. Click on the **Find or upload a sound, video or applet** to get to the **File picker**.

5. Click the **Upload a file** link and browse for Jamie's poem. Click to open it and then upload it.

6. In the next box that comes up, click **Insert**:

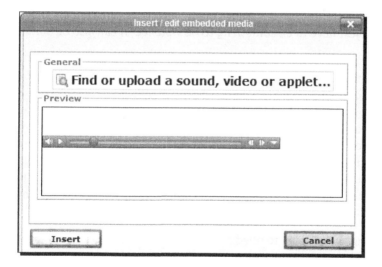

7. In the next box, click on **Save and return to course**. (Don't worry if you can't see the player anymore. It will re-appear on the course page.) Hey Presto! One really cool player with hardly any effort at all!

What just happened?

We have recorded our audio file and uploaded it to Moodle in two ways. The first way was a simple way, just as a link to the file. The second way was more attractive, embedded in its own player.

Making a film to put into Moodle

So we can do sound. Now, let's do both sound and vision! If you recall *Chapter 3, Getting Interactive*, one of the ways in which we used a database or a glossary was by enabling students to upload resources for others to see and use. If we asked them to upload their favorite photos of our class trip to a river into a Moodle database, we could make use of the pictures in the movie that we're about to create. With our new-found expertise in Audacity, we shall get one of the gang of students to record the narrative, and we shall add that to our movie. Students and parents (who have given permission for their offspring to be featured in the movie) will love to see the action and it will give the next year's hopefuls an insight into what the trip might entail.

Although we are actually making a movie (in this instance, an animated slideshow) of an event, don't think that's all you could do. With selective usage of images and text, you could create a short film to introduce a new topic. I have seen **What Happens Next?** movies on Moodle, where the story stops at a crucial point, leaving its climax open to lively discussion. A movie doesn't just have to be something to be watched; it can also be something to be learned from.

And of course, movie-making for Moodle isn't a skill restricted to the teacher. I have often booked two lessons of one hour in a computer room with classes of thirteen-year olds. In the first session, I teach the students the basics of movie-making and in the second hour, I set them an **Upload a single file** assignment, whereby they have to research, produce, and upload a movie on our current topic. We could create a movie on the Japanese Tsunami of 2011, for example. The students really enjoy it, as it makes a pleasant change from being asked to complete Word-processed tasks or prepare slideshows. Thus, just as with our podcast, once you've got the hang of film creation, why not pass on this new found knowledge to the students and let them do a better job than you did!

For movie making, we're going to need:

- A computer with a free movie-making program installed on it
- Some photographs that we have permission to use
- A sound to record (in our case, a child narrating the story of our trip to the river)

It wouldn't be a bad idea to also have a cup of coffee and a cookie with you. Well, these are not essential, but I guarantee that you'll find this a rather relaxing and a creative experience—not like real work at all!

What can we use to make our movie?

We need a really easy, powerful, and free video editing program. If you're a Mac user you will have the excellent **iMovie**, but as most users in schools tend to be tied to Windows computers, we're going to look at options for Windows XP, Vista or 7.

If you enjoy this section of the book and think you could get into this movie making game, why not be adventurous and download the free Serif Movie Plus Starter from here `http://www.serif.com/free-video-editing-software/`. We're not going to use it here as it's got more settings than we really need as beginners but it's well worth a look once you get the hang of things.

Windows XP and Windows Vista both have a free movie editing program installed as standard. It's called **Windows Movie Maker**. The Vista version is a bit different from the XP version, but they're still pretty similar. If you have a modern computer running the latest Windows 7, you can download a program called **Windows Live Movie Maker**. However, because we want to be inclusive here and make movies regardless of what operating system your computer uses (and you might not even know its operating system anyway) we are going to use an older version of Windows Movie Maker. Why? Because it will work on all those Windows systems; it's free, it's simple to work out, and it does the job!

Getting Windows Movie Maker

Let's use Windows Movie Maker to make our movie:

1. Check first if you have Windows Movie Maker already installed.

2. It might be located in **All Programs | Accessories | Entertainment | Windows Movie Maker** or it might simply be located in **All Programs | Windows Movie Maker**.

3. If you don't see it there, or if you know your computer has the Windows 7 operating system, you can download an old version of Windows Movie Maker from this link: `http://www.microsoft.com/download/en/details.aspx?id=34`.

4. You'll be presented with a screen like the following screenshot:

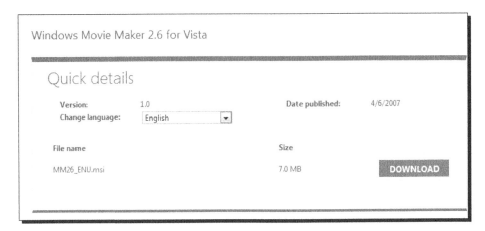

5. Click the **DOWNLOAD** button and follow the instructions. We've downloaded several programs now in previous chapters, so hopefully you should feel confident with this.

 Don't worry that the download screen only says Windows Vista. It does work on Windows 7 as well!

Time for action – creating our movie

Assuming that we now have a version of Windows Movie Maker installed on our computer, let us:

1. Find and open **Windows Movie Maker**.

2. Don't be put off by the complex look of the next screen. Consider it in four parts:
   - On the left, we have a list of tasks
   - In the middle, we have an image storage area
   - On the right, we have the preview screen
   - At the bottom, we have the film strip (timeline or storyboard) to which we'll add our images, subtitles, and commentary

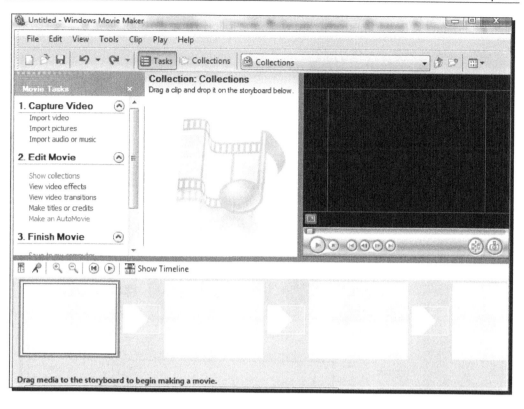

3. Click on the **Import pictures** link in the list of tasks. You'll be taken to your hard disk drive, from where you can select the photos that you want to add to the movie.

4. If you want to include all of the images from one folder, click on *Ctrl + A*, holding both keys down together.

5. Click on the **Import** button as shown in the following screenshot:

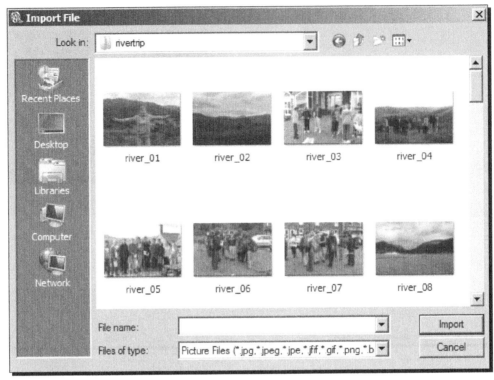

6. The images will now appear in the middle section of the Movie Maker screen, where the images are held.

7. Select one of the images (it doesn't have to be your first photo) with your cursor and drag it onto the first box of the film strip (or the storyboard). It will show on the preview screen on the right.

8. Click the **Play** button under the preview screen, on the right. Your image will play in a movie for five seconds, and then the screen will go blank. You need more photos!

Have a go hero – adding photos to the movie and testing it out

Over to you now! Select and drag the other photos into the storyboard boxes in the order in which you want them to appear in the movie. If you include the wrong image, press *Delete* on your keyboard. Then select the image that you want to appear first, press Play on the preview screen as before, and watch your movie play!

What just happened?

We used a free program, Windows Movie Maker, to make a film of a class trip to a river. We imported some still pictures—that our pupils had taken—into the program, dragged them onto a timeline, and then clicked on the Play button to preview the movie and see how it looks so far.

Improving our movie with effects and sound

Theoretically, we are done now. We can save the movie and upload it into Moodle. How quick and easy is that? But in reality, we would like to add that commentary and make it run a bit more smoothly. As you played your movie through, you probably noticed that it jerked a bit as it went from one photo to another. We can fix that. In fact, we can make the transition—from one picture to another—as simple or as sophisticated as we want. Here's how to do all this.

Time for action – adding special effects to our movie

There are two types of enhancements that we can add: **Transitions**, which make the move from one image to another, and **Effects**, which are fancy features that can be applied to our movie—such as zooming in or out, or making it look like an old, grainy film. Let's add a transition together, and then you can have a go at adding an effect.

1. From the list on the left, click on **View video transitions**.

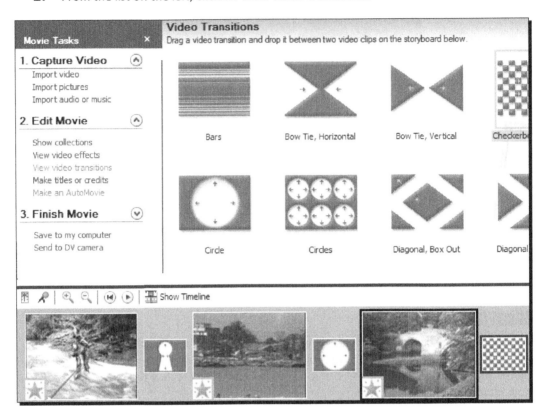

2. In the middle section of the screen, a wide selection of transitions from which you can choose will be displayed.

3. Select one transition option, with the help of your cursor, and drag it into the box between the two images on the storyboard. Three different options are shown in the previous screenshot.

4. Click the **Play** button under the preview screen to see how the transition works.

5. Add transitions between each of your images, if you wish. If you have to change your choice, click on the transition and press *Delete* on your keyboard.

 You can have lots of fun with transitions, but beware! Too many transitions can spoil a movie rather than enhance it. I tend to use just one throughout, usually the **Fade** effect, which moves smoothly from one image to the next. The same will apply to any effects that you might want to add. Sometimes less is more!

Have a go hero – make your movie zoom in and change color!

You can use just two of the many effects that are available! If you choose effects from the list on the left, you'll get a similar selection in the middle. For a single transition, you click on one transition with your cursor. But this time, you drag it onto the star located at the lower-left of the image that you want it to work on. Try an **Ease In** and a **Grayscale** and preview them. Fun, isn't it?

Once we're satisfied with our choice of transitions and effects, it's time to add the sound. When we do this, we will change the look of the film strip or the storyboard at the bottom. It will become a timeline, but not to worry, that doesn't matter. Remember, for our movie, we are using a pre-recorded (with Audacity) MP3 file of one of our girls poetically describing the trip to the river. The process would be the same if you were using some music file that you had—but keep in mind the points about copyright mentioned earlier in this chapter. Windows Movie Maker accepts different types of sound files, but the most common ones you might want to use will have `.mp3`, `.wav`, and `.wma` extensions. Sadly, you can't use your iTunes songs.

Time for action – adding sound to our movie

We have added images and effects to the image transition, but something still seems to be missing. Oh yes! How can a movie be complete without voice? Let's learn how to add sound to our movie.

1. From the list of tasks on the left, choose **Import audio or music**.

2. Select the track you want to add from your computer's hard disk drive.

3. Choose the track, and then click on **Import**, just as you did with the pictures. The imported sound file will appear in the middle section of the Windows Movie Maker screen, along with your images.

4. On the lower-left, press the drop-down arrow next to the **Storyboard**, and select **Show Timeline**. The strip will look different now as the next screenshot demonstrates. That's OK!

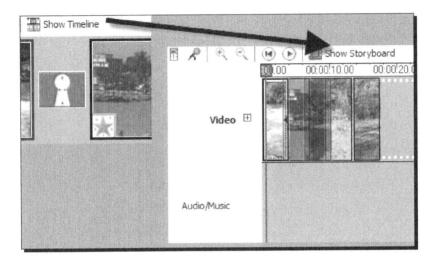

5. Select the sound clip with your cursor and drag the sound clip to the part of the timeline called **Audio/Music**.

6. You will be able to see the track underneath all of the images.

7. Click the **Play** button under the preview screen to watch and listen to your movie.

What just happened?

We've added a soundtrack to our movie by finding and importing an MP3 file, and then dragging it to the **Audio/Music** section of our movie's timeline. We can move it to the start and end it wherever we want to. However, if the audio clip is too long for our movie, we might have a problem.

Getting the sound to match our images

What if our soundtrack lasts longer than our pictures do? Of course, we can add more pictures, but what if we don't have any more pictures? Well, if it is a music clip, we can:

- ◆ Either edit it in Audacity to be the correct length and the correct bit of music and then re-import it

- ◆ Or go to the end of the music clip, click on it, and drag it to the location where the images end, as shown in the following screenshot:

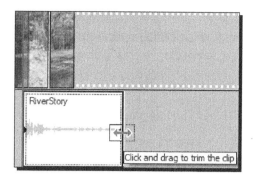

But, as it is our pupil speaking, we don't want to lose any of the lovely narrative. So, we're going to stretch out the pictures instead.

Click on an image—just as you did with the sound file—and drag it out. You'll see the number of seconds it runs for (**Duration**) increases as you drag it. Do this with all of the images until they fit the commentary.

What if our pictures last longer than our soundtrack? We can't stretch out sound as we do with still images. If it's music, we can edit it in Audacity to fit the length of the images by repeating a certain section of the music. Drag the same sound file in again, and set it to play twice (or more times).

Instead, we can click on an image and drag it inwards to make the image play for less time to shorten the audio length. However, the best method is to have just enough images and just the right length of commentary for our movie to look good. That's something that takes practice, trial, and error.

Did you notice that when you switched from **Storyboard** to **Timeline**, there was an icon for a microphone with option called **Narrate Timeline**? You can actually record a commentary as the movie is playing if you want—certainly easier for synchronizing the sound and images. We aren't going to do that here, as we've done ours in Audacity, but it's worth giving it a try some other time. Or setting it as a task for the class!

Adding the finishing touches to make our movie ready for Moodle

We are almost there! It would be nice to have opening and closing credits, just like a real movie. Then we need to save it in a way that it will work in Moodle. Let's do that now!

Time for action – adding our opening credits

To make the movie even more interesting, let's add an opening credit and a closing credit.

1. From the list on the left, choose **Make titles or credits**.

2. Choose the option **Title** at the beginning, and type in the title of the movie:

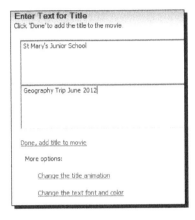

3. Watch it in the preview screen.

4. To change the way it runs, click on the **Change the title animation** link.

5. To change the type, color, and size of the text, click on the **Change the text font and color** link.

6. Click on **Done, add title to movie**.

What just happened?

We used Windows Movie Maker's titles and credits feature to add a beginning to our movie. We learned how to type in our own text and then personalize its color, font, size, and the way it runs in the movie.

 Did you notice that when you first clicked on titles and credits there were four options? Although we are just creating opening and closing credits here, you can also add captions to the actual images, or before each individual image. This is perhaps something for you and your class to experiment with in future movie creation sessions!

And now it is once more over to you.

Have a go hero – adding our closing credits

Adding closing credits works exactly in the same way as adding opening credits. You can follow the same steps as you carried out for the opening credit. However, once you reach step 2, choose **Credits at the end**. You can even have your name rolling up the screen if you wish!

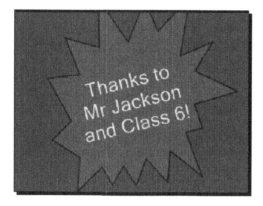

It's now time to save the movie and upload it into Moodle. The first task can be done by us, together. However, the second task can be done by you on your own!

Time for action – saving and uploading the movie into Moodle

We should really save our movie twice: once as a project file in case we want to edit it another time, as we did in Audacity, and again as a suitable movie file for Moodle.

1. Go to **File | Save Project As...** and give your movie a name. This will be the project (draft) version, which you can edit again. This should end in .MSWMM and will work only on your own computer.

2. Follow the instructions given in the following table to save the file as a finished movie.

 The save process is slightly different according to which version of Windows Movie Maker and which operating system you are using. (Use the column on the left if you downloaded our version just now). Either way, your finished file must end in .wmv.

Movie Maker 2.6 for Windows 7, Vista or XP	Movie Maker already installed on Vista
From the list of tasks on the left, choose **Finish Movie | Save to my computer**.	From the list of tasks on the left, choose **Publish**.
Name it. Browse to where you want to save it, and click on **Next**.	Name it. Browse to where you want to save it, and click on **Next**.
Click on **Show more choices | Other settings**.	Select **Compress to**.
Choose the option **Video for broadband 512 kbps**.	Check whether the estimated file space required is less than your Moodle's maximum upload limit. If not, move the compress number down.
Click on **Next** to save your movie.	

Have a go hero – displaying our movie in Moodle

No need for any more step-by-step instructions because if you can upload the MP3 file we made with Audacity, you can upload a movie too. It's done in exactly the same way. Do you remember that there were two ways to do it?

1. The first method was to go to **Add a resource \| File**.
2. The second method was (if your Moodle is set up for this) to go, **Add a resource \| Insert a label**, and then use the Moodle media (film strip) icon to embed your video. If you choose this option, it will display in a player—such as you might see on video sharing websites like **YouTube**, for example.

Summary

In this chapter, we've taken a look at how to use multimedia to showcase our students' work. We learned how to create, edit, and upload a sound file of a student reading a poem to Moodle. We discovered how to create, edit, and upload a film of a school trip to Moodle. Finally, we saw how to display our sound recording in two different ways, giving us a choice of appearance.

Additionally, and very importantly, we've also learned the basics of two programs, Audacity and Windows Movie Maker 2.6, which we can now share with our class students to inspire them to be creative. Remember the old Native American proverb: *Tell me and I'll forget. Show me and I might not understand. Involve me and I'll remember.*

In the next chapter, we shall consider more ways of using Moodle to involve our students with a rich choice of options from the world of Web 2.0.

7
Wonderful Web 2.0

In the olden days (known as Web 1.0), the Internet was all about e-mails and websites developed by professionals with pages of text that you scrolled down to read. Nowadays, the Internet is for anybody and everybody. Have you ever watched videos on YouTube? Seen photos on Flickr? Maybe even uploaded some yourself? Are you on Facebook or Twitter? You're already in the Web 2.0 world. In this chapter, we shall look at some Web 2.0 applications that can be used in Moodle—both by us teachers, and by our students. Remember—they were born into this world, so let's harness what they're used to!

In this chapter, we're going to link geography with literacy. We shall set our students a project, imagining how they'd react if their home town were flooded. We shall:

◆ Get the students to keep a blog of their experience as they work through the project

◆ Set up a Google Map of the riverside area that we're focusing on

◆ Enjoy transforming ourselves into a talking animated character to introduce the project

◆ Let the students make an online picture book of their experience

◆ Give the students a chance to summarize their project with a word cloud

All of these activities are examples of Web 2.0 applications. They are free to use and also easy to fit into Moodle. What's more, they are a lot of fun! We'll make a start shortly, but let's first understand a few basic concepts.

Web 2.0 words of warning

Apart from the Moodle blog, the rest of this chapter is about bringing the **World Wide Web (www)** inside our protected walled garden, that is Moodle. Along with the immense potential that Web 2.0 brings us come possible dangers, especially for our younger students. Thus, my suggestions will come with a few words of warning. This is not to put you off in any way, but just to help you make informed decisions about whether to use these tools or not.

Getting the pupils to blog!

The word **blog**, apparently, comes from web plus log. A blog is just an online diary or journal. Blogs are a very commonly used Web 2.0 application and there are many blogs around. But, we don't need to go outside of Moodle, as every user has his or her own space to blog, as part of their user profile. If you log into Moodle and then go to the **Navigation** block and click on **My Profile**, you will find your blog there:

Students have these settings too and they operate in just the same way as ours. These blog entries can be seen by everyone on Moodle if we choose to allow that.

It would be better though, if we can find a way quickly to see blog entries relating to our Rivers and Flooding course, rather than wading through people's blog entries on other subjects. We can do that if we add a block called **Blog menu** to our course. It allows pupils and teachers to link their blog entry to the course. Let's do it!

Time for action – adding the blog menu block so we can blog inside our course

We're going to add a block to our course page to allow students to view and add blog entries quickly and easily.

1. With the editing turned on, click on **Add a block**.

2. Choose **Blog menu**.

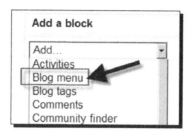

What just happened?

We added **Blog menu** to our course. Can you see the link **Add an entry about this course**? Click there and we will start the project off with a blog entry of our own.

Time for action – introducing our project with a blog entry

Let's create an introduction to our project, with the help of a blog entry.

1. Find the **Blog menu** block we just added and then click **Add an entry about this course**.

2. Click on **Add a new entry**.

3. Type a title in the **Entry title** box, and your blog entry in the **Blog entry body**, as shown in the following screenshot:

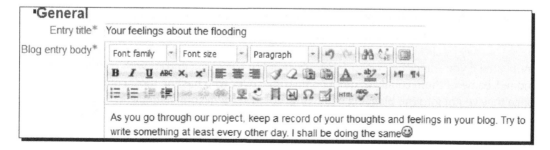

4. Scroll down and in the option **Publish To**, choose **anyone on this site**.

5. In the **Associations** section, make sure the box **Blog about course Rivers & Flooding** (or your course name) is checked.

6. Click on **Save changes**.

What just happened?

We used the blogging facility in our profile on Moodle to make a blog entry to introduce the new project to our pupils. We can add to it as we go along, specifying exactly what we'd like the students to do. Because we added our entry through the **Blog menu** block, it will be easy to find blog posts on our project. Did you notice the link **View all entries for this course**. That's where you will find your pupils' blog entries.

Words of warning

These are not really warnings, just a couple of issues that you need to be aware of.

◆ Even though we associated our blog entries to our course, they can still be seen by other people in other courses because in Moodle, blogs are attached to people, not courses. If you go to the **Navigation** block and click **Site pages | Blogs** you will see people's blog entries. Be aware, then, that the blogs in your students' profiles (and your own) aren't private to your Moodle course.

◆ You might be wondering about tags, as you scroll down to save your blog entry. Basically, a **tag** is a word connected to your interests (for us, it might be flooding) and it will link to other people on Moodle with that same tag or interest. Moodle also lets you add tags in other places—such as quizzes or your profile—so you might have noticed them there as well. If you add the **Blog tags** block (in the same way we added the **Blog menu** block) you will get a neat word cloud made up of students' interest tags. However, some schools switch off tags in case students decide to use inappropriate words, so just check with your Moodle admin first.

Have a go hero – commenting on our pupils' blogs

A blog is no use if nobody reads it. How can you prove you have read it? By adding constructive comments. Perhaps, you have read blogs on the Internet and wanted to have your say by clicking a button to contribute to the discussion? Your pupils will be very motivated if you—and their classmates—respond to their blog entries with comments. Indeed, some of them could get quite competitive over who has the most comments! So once they've got into the blogging habit, why not give them some feedback?

1. Click **View all entries about this course** from the **Blog menu** block.

2. At the bottom of a pupil's entry, click the blue **Comments** link and type your comment into the box that comes up.

3. Click on **Save comment**. Your comment will appear as in the next screenshot:

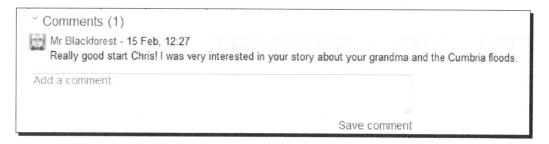

Remember to encourage the class to comment on each others' work too! (With older students, you might like to make blogging a required or assessed element of their work).

Putting a map onto Moodle

Now that our blog is up and running, we need to set the scene of the project by studying a map of the area concerned. We're going to avoid paper maps. I can never fold them back properly and my pupils are even worse! Instead, we'll use a Google Map and embed it (paste it) into Moodle. Even better, if you don't live too far from a river, you can use your own home town—they'll identify with it much better. So here we go.

Time for action – how to display a Google Map on our course page

Let's learn how to grab and display a Google Map on our Moodle course page.

1. Go to the Google Maps website (`http://maps.google.com`) and in the **Search Maps** option, type either your chosen location or a zip or postal code.

2. Once you are happy with your choice, click on the **Link** button, which is present at the top-left of your Google Map screen, as shown in the following screenshot:

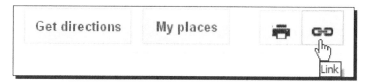

3. Click inside the option **Paste HTML to embed in website** (and don't worry about all the strange wording coming up!), and copy the text in it.

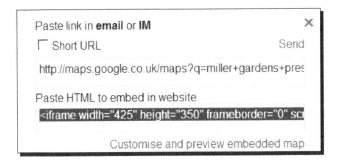

Remember, you can select the entire text by pressing *Ctrl+A*. You can copy by pressing *Ctrl+C*. You can paste by pressing *Ctrl+V*.

4. Go to your course page on Moodle, and click on **Turn editing on**.

5. Click on the **Add a resource...** menu and choose the **Page** option.

6. In the **Name** field, type the name of the map that your students need. Add a **Description** if you need to and check the box if you wish to display the description on the course page.

7. In the toolbar of the **Page content** box, click the **HTML** icon.

8. Paste (*Ctrl+V*) the text that you copied from Google Maps.

9. Scroll down and click **Update**.

10. Click on **Save and return to course**. Done!

If we now click on the name that we have given to the map—in this instance, Map of the flooding area—it opens up a new page with our map pasted (embedded) straight from Google.

But this is not just a static map! Your students can move the map around and zoom in, just as they would if they were using Google maps directly from the Internet. They can look at the satellite image instead of the conventional map. And in fact, if you make a Google account for yourself, you can add place marks, images, and even videos to the bit of the map that you are showing. However, that's not for this book to explain, but it's something to look at once you've mastered Moodle.

What just happened?

We located a map on Google of the area we're studying. We got its website link and pasted it into a text page on Moodle. As a result, the map is displayed, along with all of its features, for students to examine.

 Does the process we just went through seem familiar? We used it when embedding games in *Chapter 5*, *Games*! Embedding code from websites is not that hard, and you'll find that many so-called Web 2.0 applications work in a similar way. You merely copy and paste the code that they offer into your Moodle page to get them to show up. Make sure you remember to click the HTML icon first though, or it won't work.

Words of warning

This, again, is not really a warning, just something to be aware of when you embed maps.

Your class will love having Google maps in Moodle. Unfortunately, once they discover all of the possibilities, you might find them distracted from the task that you set. I once embedded a map of our school, and found that within a few minutes, the students had moved the map from our school to their own streets and were zooming in on the satellite view of their homes. So rather than reprimanding them, I used their interest as the starting point for a lesson on navigating with Google maps. But, you do need to be vigilant!

Introducing the project with a cartoon character

It's much more fun to set out a task with a moving and talking character than to give instructions in a word-processed document, or even by a Moodle assignment that I was encouraging you to do in *Chapter 2*, *Adding Worksheets and Resources*. We're going to make a character (or Avatar) online and, using the same principle as with the Google Map, we are going to paste or embed it into a Moodle page. We are going to use a free site where we shall make a **Voki**.

Time for action – creating a moving and a talking teacher

Let's create an animated, moving, and talking teacher and make our Moodle course learning even more enjoyable to the students.

1. Go to the website `http://www.voki.com/` and create yourself a free account.

2. Click on **Create A New Voki**, as shown in the following screenshot:

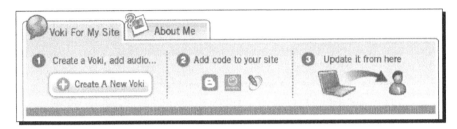

3. You will see an image and several boxes with options for editing your character.

4. In the **Customize Your Character** option, click on the **HEAD** tab. Click on the right and left arrows to choose the type of character that you want to start with (**CLASSIC** are the most conventional types). Select the gender of the character, **MALE** or **FEMALE**.

5. Scroll down to see the choices available; click on the one that you want.

6. Your chosen character will appear in the large screen to the left-hand side. Alter its features by using the **Color/Tweak** box underneath all the heads.

7. In the **Customize Your Character** option, click on the **CLOTHING** tab. As with the **HEAD** tab, click on the right and left arrows to choose the type of clothing you want for the character and then click on the item to finalize it.

8. Do the same for the **BLING** (which includes spectacles) tab.

9. Click on **DONE**, as shown in the preceding screenshot.

10. Next, click on the **Backgrounds** option. Use the arrows of the keyboard, as before, to choose a background, or click on the folder (as shown in the following screenshot) to browse and upload your own image. Click on **DONE**.

11. Now look at the **Give It A Voice** option. We're going to enter the message that is to be spoken by the computer. You can record your message on the phone, on the mike, or make one with Audacity, as we did in *Chapter 6, Multimedia*.

12. Click on the button with the image of a keyboard button named **T**. Type in your text, as shown in the following screenshot (you might need to do it phonetically to get it to sound right):

13. Select your choice in the options **Accent/Language** and **Voice**, from the menus under the text.

14. Click on the Play arrow available under the textbox to test the playback of the written text.

15. Click on **DONE**.

16. In the large screen on the left-hand side, click the Play button to preview your character.

17. When you're satisfied with it, click on **PUBLISH**.

18. Give your creation a name by entering this name in the **Name Your Scene** box.

19. Click your cursor inside the **Embed code** box and copy the words within it (like those games and Google Maps, remember?).

What just happened?

We created an account on a free site called Voki in order to generate a moving and talking character who will explain our project to the students. We chose the character's appearance and entered the words that we want the character to speak.

Have a go hero – put your Voki onto Moodle!

We've created our moving and talking teacher. Now it is time to put them on our course! If you managed to embed a Google Map into your Moodle course, then you will be able to embed a Voki as well. The process is exactly the same. Click on **Page**, click the **HTML** icon and paste the code. Have a go and do it now! Did you get something similar to the following screenshot?

If you want the Voki to appear immediately as the children access the course (as a welcome message), you can put the code into a label or in topic 0 instead of a text page. Click the **HTML** icon just as we do for a **Page**.

Words of warning

I have two important warnings for you this time:

1. When we use websites that are not connected to Moodle, there is always a possibility that they might not always be available for your course. The website owner might change the terms and conditions of the site's use, or shut down the site altogether. Web 2.0 moves at a very fast speed. Indeed, some people are even saying that the very term Web 2.0 is old fashioned these days. At the time of writing this book, the websites used in this book are very useful and stable. However, by the time you read this book, there might be better ones.

2. Do you see the advertisement underneath my Voki character (which is me, by the way!)? Because we are using a free site, it's going to have advertisements displayed, and you might worry that some are not suitable for younger children's eyes. I have been using Vokis in Moodle ever since they began and haven't had any problems. My students are used to advertisements all over the Internet and tend to ignore them and focus on the Voki. However, once again, you do need to be aware of the fact that once you are outside the safety of Moodle, there could be inappropriate content.

   The free Voki account cannot be used by children under the age of 13 so your children won't be able to make their own avatars as you have. But there is good news. Following public demand, the makers of Voki have now set up an ad-free Voki site called **Voki classroom** which you and your class can safely use and enjoy. You have to pay for this, but if the idea interests you, check out `www.voki.com/classroom`.

Telling our story through an online picture book

We're going to tell our class a tale about flooding using an online picture book maker to relate their flooding tale. When we were young, stories were told by adults or read from books. Now, **Digital Storytelling** allows us to tell our tales on the internet.

Time for action – signing up and making our picture book

Let's use a child-friendly and very beautiful site called www.storybird.com to make our book.

1. Go to the website www.storybird.com.

2. Sign up for a free Teacher account. (You'll notice that under 13 year olds can make safe accounts here too—that will be handy for us when we want them to get creative!)

3. Click on **Create**.

4. Now we need to choose a theme for the pictures we'll use in our story. We can't add our own pictures, but there are many stunning ones to choose from that artists have donated. Choose an artist that appeals to you or scroll down as I have done and click on a keyword. I am going to click on **water**:

scissors shadow shop shy silly skater snuggle sock so
strong sunset surprise thermometer torch train
vintage wait wand water weather wicked
yeti

5. This takes us to lots of pictures connected with water. Click on one you like and then click the button **Start a Storybird**.

6. Your page will be centre screen. A message will tell you where to start writing. Add your first sentence to your first page!

7. If you don't like the picture, click on any of the many others on either side of your page and drag them into your page. You have a picture on one side and a blank space to type into on the other side.

8. Add pages or remove pages by clicking the **+** or **−** signs under your page:

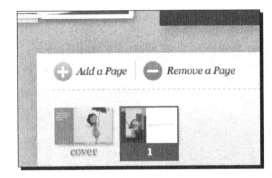

9. When you're happy with your book, click on **Menu**, which is to the top-right of the screen and then on **Publish this Storybird**.

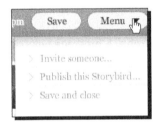

10. Choose the **Not for School** option; choose the age range and click **Publish**.

What just happened?

We created an account on a site called **Storybird** and made a picture book about a girl whose home was flooded. We saved it online and we're now going to put it into our Moodle course for our class to enjoy.

 Did you notice other options as you saved it? You don't have to make these public to the world as we did. You can keep them private for your school and you can share them just with people you know. Storybird Teacher accounts let you and your class make and share videos safely among yourselves. When you have put your first book online, why not check out what more you can do with Storybird? It's really a creative site for digital storytelling, and your colleagues might be very keen to try it out as well!

Have a go hero – add our online picture book to Moodle

We're getting used to this! Once you clicked the **Publish** button, you would have seen a link at the top-left **Embed & badges** as in the following screenshot:

Do you see some embed code as we've used before? Choose the smaller version and paste it into a Moodle Page or Label just as we did with Google maps or with the games in *Chapter 5, Games.*

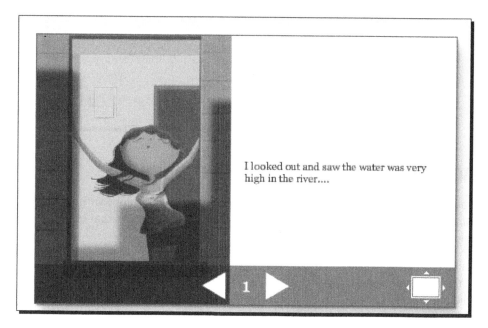

 Didn't the pages turn out beautifully? Our students will love making their own flooding stories following our example. Unfortunately, our students can't embed code as we can, but we can get them to paste the link to their Storybirds in a forum so everyone can enjoy them.

Have a go hero – setting up our Moodle Storybird forum

Yes—your turn again! After the students' efforts in making their own online picture books, we need our class to have a simple way of sharing their creation with everyone else. So we're going to set up a forum, of the single simple discussion type.

Remember how we did this in *Chapter 3, Getting Interactive*? With editing turned on, go to **Add an activity | Forum** and then select the option, **A single simple discussion**. Include instructions explaining to the students how to paste in the links to their creations. It might look something like the following screenshot:

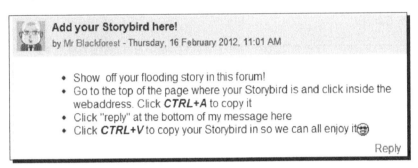

Add your Storybird here!
by Mr Blackforest - Thursday, 16 February 2012, 11:01 AM

- Show off your flooding story in this forum!
- Go to the top of the page where your Storybird is and click inside the webaddress. Click *CTRL+A* to copy it
- Click "reply" at the bottom of my message here
- Click *CTRL+V* to copy your Storybird in so we can all enjoy it

Reply

Summarizing our project in a word cloud

I had said at the start of this chapter, that we'd be combining geography with literacy. With our final Web 2.0 application, our students will not only be doing that but also arguably creating a piece of artwork.

We shall be using a tool called **Wordle**, which is a graphic representation of the most frequently used words in a blog, free write, or speech. In simple terms, it is a customizable word picture where the words used most often are the largest. It has become very popular with political analysts who use it to discover the most frequently-used words of election candidates. I have also seen it being used by teachers wishing to review the syllabus of exam boards. They enter the syllabus into Wordle to find out which topics are given more emphasis.

However, we're going to use Wordle as a medium of reflection—and also to have fun! As with our previous application, let's first create a sample exercise ourselves, so that we can speak with authority when we set our class off on the task. Do you want to see what I mean? The following screenshot shows my work in Wordle, that I created earlier:

It needs more words really, but I left it simple to encourage my class to do better! So how do we make one?

Time for action – making a Wordle word cloud

Let's learn how to create a Wordle word cloud.

1. Go to the website `http://www.wordle.net`.

2. Click on the **Create** tab.

3. Type (or paste) your words. The more often you enter a word, the bigger the word cloud will be. Click on the **Go** button.

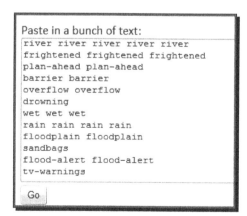

4. Change the font, color, and the layout of your created Wordle by clicking the tabs available above the word cloud, as shown in the following screenshot:

5. When you're satisfied with the word cloud, click on **Save to Gallery**.

6. Copy the link that you get for your Wordle (press *Ctrl+C* on your keyboard).

What just happened?

We used a website called Wordle to make a word cloud of the terms on our topic of flooding. The more often we typed the words, the larger they appeared in the word cloud. We chose a font and color, decided how we wanted our cloud to appear, and then saved it as a link. We will give that to our students.

Have a go hero – getting our students to send us their Wordle word clouds

I guaranteed that your students will get the idea instantly and will be very creative with its appearance. However, we want the students to benefit from this and not just play with it. So we need to make our instructions in Moodle clear to the students. Let's use a forum again, of the single simple discussion type, and let's have the students send us the link to their Wordle, as they did with their online picture book from Storybird. Here's a screenshot that shows the forum for our flooding Wordle:

Add your Wordle here!
by Mr Blackforest - Thursday, 16 February 2012, 11:08 AM

You're going to use WORDLE to make a summary of your thoughts about this project.

- Make a list of TEN words that come to your mind when doing this project
- Now put them in order of importance to you
- When you make your Wordle, write the most important one TEN times.
- Write the least important one ONCE
- and the others in between☺

Paste your link into your forum post as we did for Storybird. Here's mine but it's not very good.
http://www.wordle.net/gallery/wrdl/299477/ourfloodingproject

Reply

The students could save the Wordle as an image instead and upload it as an attachment to their forum post. To save the Wordle word cloud as an image, we need to follow a few additional steps:

1. Press the *Print Screen* button on your Keyboard (Windows) when your Wordle is finished.

2. Go to **All Programs | Accessories | Paint** and press *Ctrl + V* on your keyboard to paste your Wordle image.

3. Go to **File | Save as** and choose **.jpg** file.

4. On a Mac computer, press *Command+Shift+3* to save your image as a `.png` file onto your desktop.

Words of warning

Nothing new this time—just a reminder.

When we and our students save the Wordle to the gallery, it becomes visible to the world at large. So names with address or anything incriminating should not be entered. Equally, there will be Wordle images on the site with inappropriate content if your students look hard enough. However, many teachers across the globe use Wordle successfully. I have yet to hear of a student being traumatized by it. But it's your call.

Summary

In this chapter, we mainly ventured outside of the walled garden that is Moodle, and entered the wonderful world of Web 2.0. This has enabled us to add creativity and more interactivity to our Moodle course by getting our students to blog and comment on each other's entries, embedding a Google Map into our course and creating a moving, talking teacher with Voki (as a refreshing change from ourselves!) We also introduced them to Digital Storytelling with Storybird and channeled their literary and artistic creativity with Wordle.

We've had a lot of fun in the last three chapters. However, if we want to make our Moodle course successful and long-lasting, we need to ensure that everything we put on it actually works for us and our students. Not as obvious as you might assume, but of vital importance. Now that we have got plenty of skills under our belt, in the next chapter, we shall have a look at the practicalities and the nitty-gritty of Moodle!

8
Practicalities

This chapter is about the 'nitty-gritty of uploading and displaying our materials in Moodle. We need to ensure that everything works for our pupils and teaching colleagues. I don't mean this in a technical sense with respect to the Internet connection—that's our admin's job. However, we have to be certain about our worksheets, slideshows, photos, and other resources—all of which should be easily accessible regardless of the type of computer that people use.

In this chapter, we're going to help a student, Joe, who can't view our worksheets and PowerPoint presentations at home. We're also going to advise a colleague, Liz, who is new to Moodle and wants help with displaying her teaching materials. We shall:

- Provide our students with an alternative way of viewing worksheets and slideshows if they don't have Microsoft Word or PowerPoint
- Learn how to display word-processed files in a way everyone can see them
- Make it easier for our classes to watch our slideshow presentations
- Investigate how best to upload and display photos on Moodle
- Find out how to show YouTube videos on our course even though YouTube is banned in school
- Look at how Moodle can best work with the latest mobile devices such as iPhones and iPads.

Miss, I can't do the homework because I haven't got Word at home!

Many of us, even without thinking about it, create worksheets in Microsoft Office Word and presentations in Microsoft Office PowerPoint. This might be because our school has a license for them and they are installed on our computers. However, they don't always come for free when you purchase a desktop computer or a laptop. Sometimes, you may have to buy them separately. I know several of my students who don't have these programs at home. But, I refuse to accept the excuse from our pupil Joe for not having completed his home work because there is a free alternative!

LibreOffice is a suite of applications for word processing, spreadsheets, presentations, and so on, that anyone can download and use. It is also suitable if you have a Mac instead of a Windows-based computer. If you have LibreOffice, you can view files created in MS Office, even though you don't have MS Office. Students can upload their work using LibreOffice's equivalent of Word, and Moodle will be happy to accept them. We're going to download it for use and then put a link to the site on our course page so that the students can download it at home.

 Like Moodle, LibreOffice is also an open source. This means that anyone is welcome to help in improving both Moodle and LibreOffice, as the code that makes them work is available for people to adapt and offer to the rest of the world for free. True global collaboration!

Time for action – getting a free alternative to Microsoft Office

Students who don't have MS Office installed in their computer can search the Internet for some software application that supports MS Office created files. One such application is LibreOffice. Let's learn how to download it.

1. Go to the website `http://www.libreoffice.org/`.

2. Click on **Download LibreOffice**.

3. Look at the number of the latest, feature-rich version. At the time of writing, it was 3.5.0 but it might be different when you read this.

4. Scroll down to the drop-down boxes and choose your type of computer operating system. They're usually clever enough to guess, so it will probably already give you the correct type. Mine here says Windows, British English, which is correct.

5. Click the first link to download it.

6. When the next screenshot comes up, click on **Run**. (If you have only the save file link, that's OK. Save it and then run it.)

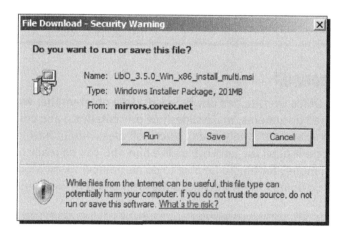

7. If you get a security warning prompting you to agree to the installation, go ahead and agree.

8. Click on **Next** to install LibreOffice.

9. Keep clicking on **Next**, following their instructions, until you get to the following screenshot, and then click on **Finish**.

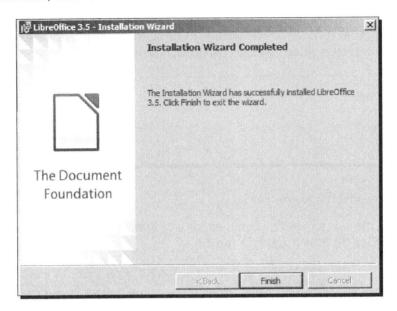

What just happened?

We visited the LibreOffice website and downloaded a free program that will enable us to create word-processed documents, make slideshow presentations, and create spreadsheets. The program will let us and our students edit Microsoft files without having Microsoft Office on our computer. For our pupil Joe, and others like him, this can be really handy. His parents don't need to spend money for him to be able to do his homework on Moodle. His parents just need to let him download the LibreOffice suite! This is where you come in.

Have a go hero – giving our students an alternative to Microsoft Office

Our first step in downloading of LibreOffice was to go to `http://www.libreoffice.org/`. Why not provide a link at the top of our Moodle course? If we do this, the pupils can download the software directly from our Moodle site. You could:

◆ Either edit **Topic 0** and add the link to LibreOffice as a hyperlink
◆ Or click on **Add a resource | URL** to provide a short description with a link to LibreOffice, as shown in the following screenshot:

Rivers and flooding -what's it all about?

Click here to go to the National Geographic Kid's site

 LibreOffice - a free program

Don't have Word? Don't have PowerPoint? Click the link

LibreOffice works in a very similar way to Microsoft Word, and you and your students will soon get the hang of it. You might notice, however, that when the students send their work to you in a Moodle assignment, the last few letters of the filename (the file extension) are different from what we might expect. Let's take a step back for a moment and look at some of the file extensions that our worksheets might have:

File extension	What it is
.docx	A Microsoft Word 2007 or 2010 document. If you don't have MS Office, you can open it in LibreOffice (if you don't have the 2007 or 2010 version, you can ask the student to save as a 97-2003 file).
.doc	An older Microsoft Word (such as Word 97 or Word 2003) document.
.wps	Microsoft Works document. Sometimes, instead of Microsoft Word, this program comes free with new PCs . If you choose **File** | **Save as** you can save the file as a Word document (you can also download **Word Viewer**).
.odt	A LibreOffice word-processed document.
.pdf	The sort of file that you have to open with Adobe Acrobat Reader. You can't easily edit it, but it can at least be opened on all computers. (See the following topic for more information.)

Choosing the best file type for Moodle

As I said earlier, uploading our worksheets into Moodle isn't as simple as we first thought. The situation could be such that we've got Word 2010, but our students only have Word 2003. It could also be that we've got Word 2007, and the students don't have any version of Microsoft Office at all. Or they only have Microsoft Office created documents on their computer, but do not have Microsoft Office installed. Using LibreOffice can be very helpful to you in such cases. However, as teachers there is another possibility.

Our colleague, Liz, wants to know the best way to display her worksheets in Moodle, without much effort. Her worksheets are a mixture of .doc, .odt, and .docx depending on the computer she works on. As she wants the students to only view her materials and not download or edit them, what I'd suggest to her is that she save her material as .pdf files.

PDF stands for **Portable Document Format** and is a type of file that works on different computers and with different operating systems. Use it if you merely need your students to read a resource and not alter it.

Almost everyone has a program called **Adobe Reader**, which opens these `.pdf` files. Thus, people will be able to view Liz's materials with no difficulty. Let's look at how Liz (and we) can do this, using a homework resource on the Mississippi, which she has stored as a `.docx` file.

Adobe Reader is a software program that is usually present on people's computers. Why not provide a link to download it on your course page just like the one that we created for OpenOffice? You should link to `http://www.adobe.com/products/reader/`.

Time for action – saving a Rivers homework as a .pdf file for ease of access on Moodle

As we know, not everybody will have the MS Office software installed on their computer. So for the files that we want the users to only read and not edit, we can save the file as a PDF file. Let's learn how to do this.

1. Open LibreOffice on your computer (you might have an icon on the desktop).

2. Click on **Open...** and browse and select the file that you want to open using the LibreOffice software just as you would for Moodle.

3. The file will open up in LibreOffice.

4. Click on **File** and then click on **Export as PDF...**, as shown in the following screenshot:

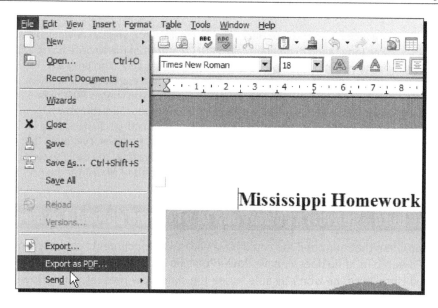

5. On the next screen, click on **Export**.

6. Select where you want the file saved to, and then click on **Save**.

What just happened?

We used a built-in feature of LibreOffice to create a different version of Liz's homework sheet, which can be read on many different types of computer. We opened up the document (that had been created in Microsoft Word 2010) and exported it as a .pdf file. You can see the result in the following screenshot:

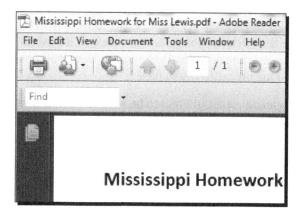

If you don't want to use LibreOffice to create a PDF, you can download a free (open source) program called **PDFCreator** from the website http://sourceforge.net/projects/pdfcreator/. This program acts like a printer. You create your worksheet in a Word document, then instead of choosing your usual (real-life) printer you choose PDFCreator, and it will generate a PDF version of the file for you. Sometimes, while converting documents into PDF, the layout (formatting) changes, so you check this before uploading your file to Moodle. However, I've found that PDFCreator is very good at maintaining the formatting. You can also save documents as PDF with the more modern versions of MS Word.

Have a go hero – convert a PowerPoint to a PDF and upload it to Moodle

The same problem that our pupil Joe could have with Word documents could also occur with Microsoft PowerPoint. If he doesn't have PowerPoint on his home computer and if he hasn't downloaded LibreOffice, he won't be able to see the slideshow presentations. However, LibreOffice will convert these slideshows into .pdf just as quickly. Try it, and then use **Add a resource** | **File** to upload the PDF file into Moodle!

Making it easier for our students to view our slideshows

Didn't you just do that? Well, yes. One way to ensure that our wonderful presentations are accessible to all our students, irrespective of their home set up, is to convert the presentation into .pdf files.

However, a .pdf file is pretty static. It won't include any animations, sound, or video. It basically takes an interactive slideshow and converts it into an online paper version. Not good enough. Our colleague Liz has spent a long time on her PowerPoint presentations, and she is not keen on losing their effects. We're going to work with her on a slideshow that she created on the New Orleans floods, and ensure that it stays as jazzy on Moodle as it is offline! To do this, we shall download yet another free application—which converts PowerPoint slideshows into interactive **Flash** files.

You don't need to know anything about Flash to be able to do this. However, it's worth noting that you and your students need to have a recent version of the Flash player installed on your computer in order for the application to work (just as you need Adobe Reader to view PDF files). And, as we shall see later, Flash doesn't work with all devices. If you're lucky enough to have a set of iPads for your class for instance, this won't work. Let's take it one step at a time.

Time for action – getting a program that displays our interactive presentations

Let's download a program that will convert our PowerPoint slideshows into interactive Flash files.

1. Go to the website `http://www.ispringsolutions.com`.

2. Find the image as in the next screenshot and click on the **Download iSpring Free** arrow.

3. You'll be asked to sign up for a free account. Agree—it's OK and will give you access to the download box.

4. If you are using Internet Explorer and are prompted to **Run** or **Save**, click on **Run**. If you are using Firefox, you will only get the **Save File** option. Click on it, save the file, and then open it. (If you were wondering, `.msi` stands for **Microsoft Installer**.)

5. If asked whether you want to run the software, agree and click on **Run**!

6. In the setup wizard, click on **Next**.

7. Agree to the terms and conditions, and then click on **Next** until the software is installed.

8. Click on **Finish**. The application will open up and prompt you to **Launch PowerPoint**.

What just happened?

We went to the iSpring Solutions website and downloaded a free program that will convert our PowerPoint presentations to a little Flash movie that will play nicely in Moodle, with our animations included. The free program is named iSpring Free. In future, we just need to go to PowerPoint and there will be a toolbar present to save our presentation using iSpring. If you have hundreds of animations, it might not save them all; but are you sure hundreds of animations is a good idea anyway?

Time for action – saving our slideshow so that everyone can see it

By everyone I mean all pupils and teachers—whether or not they have MS Office or LibreOffice! We're going to open up Liz's New Orleans PowerPoint slideshow, save it in Flash format, and then upload it into Moodle. Let's learn how it is done.

1. Open up PowerPoint and open the presentation that you want to convert.

2. From the iSpring free tab at the top, click on **Publish**.

3. On the next screen, select or deselect the **Start presentation automatically** option according to your wish.

4. Click on the **Publish** button again.

What just happened?

We've just converted a regular PowerPoint to a fancy Flash movie that will work on all of our pupils' computers! Having downloaded and installed the iSpring program, we simply needed to open up our presentation and publish it into Flash format. You'll find that no matter which format your new file is initially saved in, it will end up in the `.swf` format. This is yet another file extension, which tells us that the file is a Flash file. This is the one to go on our course page.

Have a go hero – uploading and displaying our new slideshow in Moodle

There's nothing magical about this next step. Instead of uploading Liz's PowerPoint slideshow on the New Orleans floods, we're going to upload the `.swf` file made for us by iSpring. You can try saving a PowerPoint slideshow that you've created (preferably with some animations so that you can see them work). If you use the same file that you earlier converted to `.pdf`, you'll be able to compare and contrast the two versions. Then go to your Moodle course and click on **Turn editing on**. Then go to menu option **Add a resource | File**, upload the file, and display it. Our New Orleans one looks like this:

Can you see that the slideshow comes with its own little player? This is neat! Another improvement over displaying it as a regular slideshow is the fact that it opens up with one click and doesn't waste a lot of the students' time. Using a regular slideshow students might face problems, such as first seeing a message asking *Do you want to open or save this file?*, then having to decide on *Yes* or *No*, then opening the file, and finally discovering that they can't view it because they don't have the correct version of Microsoft PowerPoint.

Making sure that all of our images look correct on Moodle

Haven't we already done this in *Chapter 1, Getting Started*? Uploaded photos? Yes, but we're just going to do some tweaking now—especially as Liz has some images that she'd like to display. She has a folder of photos from her cousin who was actually in New Orleans at the time of the traumatic flooding in 2005. Liz wants to display the folder of photos and wants to use one of them, smaller in size, in the label to introduce her materials. So we need to look at how to resize photos.

It is better to resize your photos before you upload them into Moodle. If you use the **handlebar** in the HTML editor to resize a photo, the image could appear distorted. If you change its dimensions online, the image might look smaller even though the file size is still as large. Think of it as a song. Both the lyrics as well as the music last only for three minutes. However, if you're told you can have only one minute of music, but you still have to fit in the three minutes of lyrics, it just wouldn't be right, would it? Similarly, if you try to resize your photo once it's uploaded, it would not be right! So we'll do it the proper way.

But first, let's take a quick look at what we actually mean when we say image. As with word-processed documents, images can come in different types depending on whether they are photographs, cartoon type pictures, or animated clips that you sometimes see on web pages. Each type of image is recognized by its file extension. The most common ones are:

Image type	What it is
.jpg	The most common photo format. Make sure that your photos are of this type.
.gif	The most common format for graphic images, clipart/cartoons, or animated images.
.png	Another popular format for images, especially on websites.
.bmp	A high-quality picture file, not really suited for Moodle due to its size. Avoid it.

Time for action – getting a program to help us edit images for Moodle

For this purpose, we need a simple program that will change the size of our photos or other images without losing their quality or distorting them.

If you are using a Mac, you will have a facility known as **Preview**, which does the job we want.

If you have Microsoft Office, there is a very basic image editing program called **Microsoft Picture Manager**, which is worth trying out.

However, if you are on a PC and don't have Microsoft Office installed in your computer, there is a free program that we're about to use. This program will resize the single photo Liz wants in her label. Furthermore, Liz can show the students all of the photos in the folder at one go. It's called **IrfanView**.

1. Go to the website `http://www.irfanview.com/`.

2. Click on the IrfanView download link, as shown in the following screenshot:

3. Next, click on the button named **Download Now**. If you get a message saying that downloading files is blocked, click on the message and then click on **Download file**.

4. Click on **Run** (if you only have the **Save** option, that's fine too!). If you're prompted to allow this, go ahead and agree. It's perfectly safe!

5. Keep clicking on **Next**, until you get to the following message:

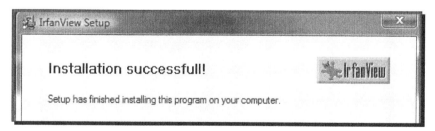

6. Click on **Done**, and you should be taken to IrfanView. If not, click on the icon available at your desktop.

What just happened?

We went to the IrfanView website and downloaded a free program that will enable us to alter the dimensions of photos and other images that we want to use in Moodle. IrfanView can also edit photos in many other ways. However, we don't have time to investigate all of these. But why not have a look at its other features once you've mastered the resizing?

Time for action – resizing a single photo to display on Moodle

Make sure that you have a reasonably large photo ready. Using IrfanView, let's make the image smaller.

1. Start IrfanView.

2. Select menu option **File | Open**.

3. As with Moodle, navigate to the photo that you want (that ends with the extension .jpg), select it, and click on **Open**.

4. Click on the **Image** tab and then click on **Resize/Resample**. The following dialogue box will appear:

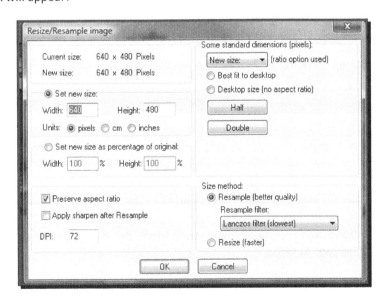

5. If you understand about pixels, you can change the number of pixels in the **Width** box. The height will change accordingly, to ensure that the image is not distorted.

6. If you prefer to think in centimeters (**cm**) or inches, click on that unit and then change the width.

7. If you wish to make your photo a certain percent smaller than it was before, click on **Set new size as percentage of original**, and specify the required percentage.

8. Click on the **OK** button located at the bottom of the window.

9. Select menu option **File | Save as** and (if you want) rename your photo or save over the original.

What just happened?

We used the free program IrfanView to transform a larger image into a smaller image—but, without spoiling its appearance. By selecting the **Preserve aspect ratio** checkbox (as shown in the previous screenshot) we ensured that if we decreased the width, the height would decrease accordingly. You can deselect this checkbox and choose your own width and height ratio, but your photo might look a bit odd. We now have a photo suitably resized for Moodle.

Have a go hero – proving the importance of resizing images!

Not convinced? Think it's a lot of effort when you can just upload your photo as it is and change it in Moodle? Well, try a little experiment then.

◆   Upload the largest photo that you have (thousands of pixels, hopefully!) and display it in a Moodle label, resizing it to around 100 x 100 pixels.

◆   Then go to IrfanView and resize that same photo properly, to around 100 x 100 pixels. Then upload it and display it in a second label.

Notice any differences? If you have a super-fast broadband connection, you might not notice much. However, at the very least, you will find that it takes more time to upload the image first and then resize it, as compared to using IrfanView and then uploading the resized image. Seconds maybe, but as a busy teacher, you can get impatient with every extra moment wasted.

If you look closely at the first photo, you will probably see that it looks a bit—well—squashed. The second version is clearer. That's because in the first one, we are singing a three-minute song to a one-minute tune whereas in the second one, the tune and lyrics are both one minute!

Finally, and most important of all, if your Internet connection is not that fast, or if any of your students are on dial-up, the first photo will take ages to appear, a bit at a time, whereas the second one, properly resized, will be displayed almost immediately.

Ok, so let's now look at resizing a whole folder of photos, such as Liz's cousin's ones. It would be a pain to have to go through the previous process for every single image; fortunately it isn't necessary with IrfanView.

Time for action – re-sizing several photos, all in one go

Let's learn how to re-size several photos at once.

1. Start IrfanView.

2. Select menu option **File | Batch conversion/Rename**.

3. In the dialogue box that appears next, click on **Look in** and navigate to the folder of photos that you want to resize.

4. Click on the folder. The images will appear individually.

5. Click on the **Add all** button. Their filenames will appear in the **Input files** box at the bottom of the screen:

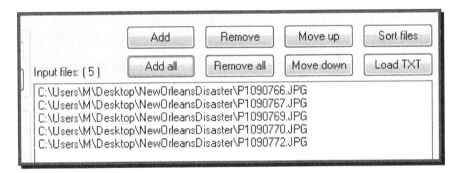

6. In **Output directory for result files**, choose the location to which you want the folder of resized photos to be saved. If you want it in the same place as the current folder, click on **Use current ('look in') directory**.

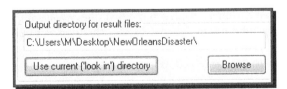

7. Under **Batch conversion settings**, click on **Advanced**.

8. In the box that is displayed, set your new size, and ignore everything else!

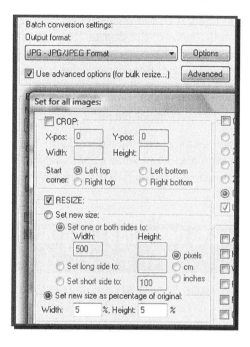

9. Click on **OK**.

10. Back on the main screen, click on **Start Batch**.

11. Sit back and relax as IrfanView does all the work of resizing your photos for you!

What just happened?

We used IrfanView to resize a whole folder of photos for Moodle. Now when we upload them it will take less time, and they will display better—especially for those of our students whose Internet connection isn't as fast as ours.

There are several ways to have photo slideshows in Moodle. Your Moodle might have its own gallery such as **Lightbox Gallery**. If it doesn't, you might consider using an online gallery such as **Flickr**, although you'd have to be careful if you are using images of children. Our colleague Liz is simply going to display them as a folder for the time being.

Showing YouTube videos on Moodle when YouTube is banned

Here's another practical problem that Liz has presented us with: she's found a couple of really good eye witness amateur videos of the disaster. She's got permission from the owner (*very important*) to use them in her Moodle course, but she can't show them because our school won't allow us to access YouTube! How do we solve that one?

The answer is to wait until we get home and then download the video onto our own computer. Then we can upload it as a regular file into our Moodle course.

There are several ways of downloading YouTube videos. Some of them require you to install something on your own computer, while others ask you for an e-mail address to send you the video. But the one we're going to use here gives us the video pretty much instantaneously.

Time for action – how to download a YouTube video to use on Moodle

Make sure that you have permission to do this! Carefully read YouTube's advice on copyright issues at `http://www.youtube.com/t/copyright_center`.

1. Find your YouTube video and copy (*Ctrl+C*) its web address (URL) as shown in the following screenshot:

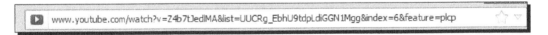

2. Go to the website `http://mediaconverter.org`.

3. Click the icon **Enter a link**.

4. Paste (*Ctrl+V*) that video address into the input box, as shown in the following screenshot:

5. Click on **OK** and then on **Go to the Next Step**.

6. Click the drop-down arrow for **---select a file type---** and choose **flv**.
   (You could choose another type, such as **wmv**, but this one will do for us.)

7. Click on **Next step** and ignore the next page of instructions.

8. Click on **Start**.

9. Sit back and relax while the site does its job!

10. Click on the **download** link to download the video to somewhere that you can store
    it ready for Moodle.

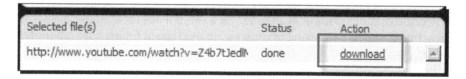

What just happened?

We used a free website service that enabled us to download in five steps a YouTube video
that we can now upload to our Moodle course. We found our video's URL on YouTube,
entered it on this site, and received a link to the file.

 There are many different sites that will let you download YouTube videos if you
have permission to. If you're not happy with **mediaconverter**, try one of these two
sites: http://www.zamzar.com or http://www.youconvertit.com.

Did you notice while going through the process that many different video (and audio) file
types were on offer? As we've looked at document file extensions and image file extensions,
now might be a good time to cast a glance at the type of multimedia file Moodle prefers.
Here's a simple table explaining the most common formats. There are others, but these are
the ones that we're most likely to want to use.

File extension	Sound/video?	How useful is it for us in Moodle?
.flv	Video	A flash video file such as those you get on YouTube. Plays well if you have multimedia filters enabled but it doesn't appear in Apple devices like iPads, iPhones, or iPods.
.wmv	Video	The kind of file we made with Windows Movie Maker.
.avi	Video	A large video file type. Moodle will play it, but it's too big, really!
.mpg	Video	Tends to be quite small in size. You'll need **Quicktime.**

File extension	Sound/video?	How useful is it for us in Moodle?
`.mov`	Video	An Apple video file. Can be quite large. You'll need Quicktime.
`.mp4`	Video	Another, small, Apple file. You'll need Quicktime.
`.mp3`	Sound	The best sound file format for Moodle. We set up Audacity for these.
`.wav`	Sound	A Windows sound file. These can be large and won't play in the player.

Using Moodle on your i-devices

More and more classes these days are using iPads or iPod touches. As I write, my school's Assistant Headteacher has just put in an order for a set of iPads for the Special Educational Needs department and he is thinking of ordering an iPod touch for each member of the teaching staff. (Yes, please!)

Many teachers and a fair number of older students also have iPhones. If you, as a teacher, think you might be doing a lot of uploading through your iPhone, you might like to download the official Moodle iPhone app from the iPhone store. (It's free.) If you have a Blackberry or an Android phone, don't feel left out, because they also have a free app available here: `http://moodle.org/plugins/view.php?id=175`.

Here's a quick checklist of the pros and cons of mobile devices such as iPads.

What's good

Here are some advantages of iPads and similar devices:

- It's really easy for you to keep track of forum posts while you're out and about.
- It's useful for assessing children's work while you are moving around the classroom. Much less intimidating for them if you come with your iPad to their desk than if you summon them to your desk at the front to discuss their grades.
- Children themselves can pass the device around their table, taking it in turns to answer quiz questions, for example, to develop their team work skills.
- If they have iPods, children can take photos of their project work and upload them to their private files on Moodle for use later.

What's not so good

Here are some disadvantages of iPads and similar devices:

♦ IPads, iPhones, and iPods don't work with Flash, so our XML games won't display.

♦ Our FLV videos downloaded from YouTube won't display—but if that's going to be a problem for your school, you can choose a different format before downloading.

♦ A lot of SCORM activities contain Flash and so they won't work either. Our great **Fling the Teacher** game from *Chapter 5, Games*, will have to be played on a computer, sadly.

♦ If you or your students are doing a lot of text-based work, typing on the built-in keyboard is not as easy as on a computer.

♦ Our fantastic iSpring slideshow converter won't work and if we use LibreOffice to convert it to a `.swf` file, that won't work either. We could still convert our slideshow to a `.pdf` file, or if you have PowerPoint 2010, why not turn your slideshow into a movie by converting it to a `.mp4` file?

Summary

In this chapter, we've focused on making sure that everything on our course page displays properly for our students. We've also helped a new Moodler ensure that her teaching materials are easily accessible. We have provided a link on our course page to LibreOffice —a free alternative to MS Office—for students such as Joe, who don't have Microsoft Office Word at home. We used LibreOffice's PDF conversion facility to change documents into a format that anyone can easily read. After that, we downloaded and used iSpring, a free program that converts slideshows to a format that the children can view without difficulty on their computers. We also downloaded an image resizing and editing program, IrfanView, to help colleague Liz display her photos better on Moodle. Then we learned how to get YouTube videos onto Moodle, even though the site is not allowed in our school. Finally, we investigated potential problems with viewing Moodle activities on Apple devices such as iPads.

We can be happy in the knowledge that even though Joe's Internet connection is slow, and he doesn't have MS Office, he'll still be able to view his teacher's resources. And he'll have no excuse for not doing his homework! Now we have sorted out the practicalities of our course, we're ready to go that one step further. In the final chapter, we'll check out some advanced activities.

9
Advanced Tips and Tricks

This chapter gives a taste of Moodle level two! It looks at how we can use the more advanced features of Moodle to enhance our teaching further. The previous chapters contained everything that you need to build and run a fully interactive Moodle course. However, once you're familiar with those resources and activities, you might want to read the following pages to stretch your skills a little more.

In this chapter, we're going to complete our course by:

◆ Challenging our students' newly acquired knowledge through a decision-making exercise

◆ Getting the students to complete the evaluation of an entire course to help us review it for the next year

We're going to find out how we can use Moodle's optional extras to:

◆ Direct their learning step by step so that they move on only when we feel they're ready to tackle the activities

◆ Give them certificates, word games, photo galleries, and more

And finally, we're going to:

◆ Revamp our course homepage to make it look more like a traditional web page—believing in the phrase: *Appearance is Everything*!

Using Moodle to get our students to make decisions

Have you ever done any of those fun online quizzes that abound, such as *How attractive are you?*, *Which famous person do you most resemble?*, and so on? They start by asking you questions such as *Are you male or female?* and then tailor their answers to suit your selection. These activities work by having alternative **branches** depending on what we choose each time we click on one of the buttons. If you are good at slideshow presentations, you can do similar kinds of things by hyperlinking an action button to a particular slide. Moodle has this branching feature too, in the **Lesson** module. We're going to use it now to create a decision-making exercise for our students. It's great for those higher level thinking skills that we're meant to encourage in the students. We are going to ask our class to put themselves in the shoes of a nine year old girl, Milly, who is about to experience a major flood in her road. The students have to make choices for her and her family according to what they have learned about the dangers of flooding. What they choose will have an effect on Milly's safety—and their score!

 A Moodle Lesson is not what we think of as a lesson in the literal sense! It is a series of connected pages that you'll use to direct the students through a certain course of action. It can be used for DMEs, for step-by-step independent learning, or for other activities requiring linking sections. It is very complex to set up. We are only touching its surface here.

Time for action – creating a decision-making exercise (DME)

Let's create a **Decision Making Exercise** (**DME**) which will test the decision-making skills and spontaneity of the students.

1. With editing turned on in the topic section you want, click on **Add an activity** and then click on **Lesson**.

2. In the **Name** box, give a title to your exercise, which your students will click on to start the exercise.

3. For our basic activity, set the **Maximum number of answers** to **2** and the **Maximum grade** to **10**, as shown in the following screenshot. Use other numbers when you try it out yourself some other time!

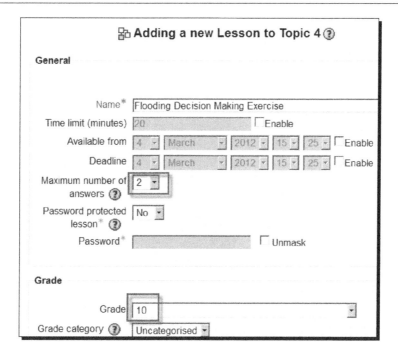

4. From the **Display ongoing score** drop-down menu, select **Yes**.

5. Ignore everything else! This is just a taster, remember.

6. Click on **Save and display**. You'll get the screen as shown in the following screenshot:

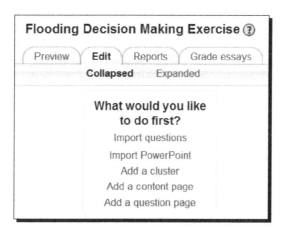

Make sure you are in **Collapsed** view. If the word **Collapsed** is not clickable; you are OK. If you can click on **Collapsed**, then click on it before you continue.

7. Click on the **Add a content page** link.

8. Enter a scene-setting introduction in the **Page contents** box, as shown in the following screenshot:

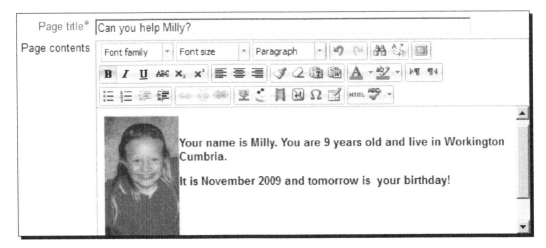

9. In the **Description** box of **Content 1**, type a short phrase and from the **Jump** menu, choose **Next page**.

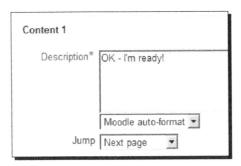

10. Scroll down and click on the **Add a question page** link.

11. In the **Actions** block on the next screen, click on the **Add a new page...** drop-down menu and select the **Question** option.

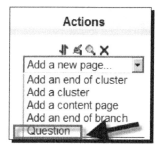

12. Select the **Multiple choice** question type and click on **Add a question page**.

13. In the **Page title** box, enter a question. (This title is just for your reference; students won't see it.)

14. In the **Page contents** box, specify the first decision to be made, as shown in the following screenshot:

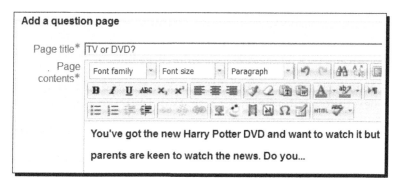

15. In the **Answer 1** box and the **Response 1** box, enter an answer and your feedback for it, respectively.

16. In the **Answer 2** box and the **Response 2** box, enter another answer and your feedback for it, respectively.

17. For **Score 1** and **Score 2**, set the correct answer to **1** and the incorrect answer to **0**.

18. Set **Jump 1** and the **Jump 2** to **Next page**.

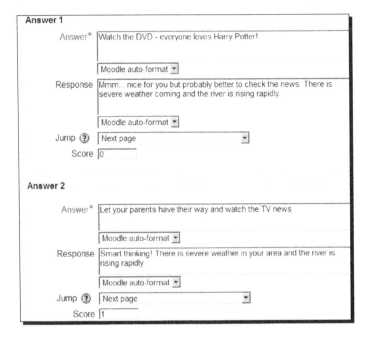

19. Scroll down and click on the **Add a Question Page** button.

20. In the **Actions** block on the next screen, click on the **Add a new page...** drop-down menu next to your last page (in our case, **TV or DVD?**) and select **Question**.

21. Select the **Multiple choice** question type and click on **Add a question page**.

22. In the **Page title** block, enter a short title (just for your reference).

23. In the **Page contents** block, set out the decision to be made, as shown in the following screenshot:

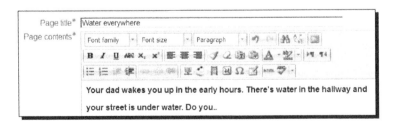

24. In the **Answer 1** box and the **Response 1** box, enter an answer and your feedback for it, respectively.

25. In the **Answer 2** box and the **Response 2** box, enter another answer and your feedback for it, respectively.

26. For **Score 1** and **Score 2** set the correct answer to **1** and the incorrect answer to **0**.

27. Set both **Jump 1** and **Jump 2** to **Next page**.

Answer 1

Answer* | ignore him and go back to sleep?

Moodle auto-format

Response | Bad idea. The water has risen three feet in an hour and a half. You need to get up!

Moodle auto-format

Jump ⑦ | Next page

Score | 0

Answer 2

Answer* | go and rescue your DVD

Moodle auto-format

Response | Nice try but your DVD is soaked beyond repair. Your house is flooded. The water has risen three feet in an hour and half. Well done at least for getting up to help your parents sort out the mess

Moodle auto-format

Jump ⑦ | Next page

Score | 1

28. Scroll down and click on the **Add a Question Page** button.

What just happened?

Phew! Let's just take a break for a moment.

We used the Lesson module to set up a decision-making exercise (DME). We asked our students to put themselves in the place of a girl in the North of England whose house was flooded a few years back. This role play is based on a true story and so at the end of my lesson I actually linked the story on the BBC News website to our Moodle course, so that my students could see that their decision making had been done for real.

We used a content page to set the scene and we linked it to a multi-choice question page where we gave the students two options, depending on which they are given some appropriate feedback from us, and a score of either **0** or **1**. We linked both choices to another question and repeated the process.

So far, we have had two choices and two points. We need to carry on until we feel that enough action has been taken. Our DME is given a score out of 10.

Have a go hero – carry on decision making!

When we clicked on the **Add a question page** link, we got to a screen similar to the one shown in the following screenshot:

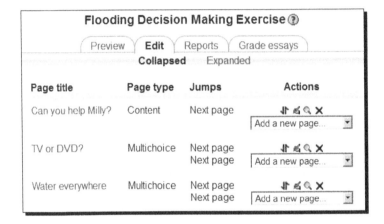

- In the **Actions** block, click on **Add a new page** next to your last page (in our case, **Water everywhere**) and select **Question** from the drop-down list.
- Choose **Multiple choice**.
- Add another decision with its answers, responses, and scores.
- Keep going!
- Why not make a couple of scores more than 1?

Time for action – finishing and viewing our DME

Once we're satisfied with the activity, it's time for a final page—rounding it all off. Here's how:

1. In the **Actions** block, link your last question page to a Content page.

2. Prepare the summary as shown in the following screenshot:

3. In the **Description** box of **Content 1** provide a goodbye comment.

4. From the **Jump** drop-down, choose **End of lesson** and then click the **Add a question page** link as usual.

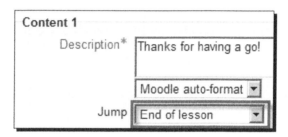

5. On the next screen, click the **Preview** tab to test that all of the connected pages work. Try the alternative answers—does it all follow on appropriately?

6. Go to your course page; switch to **Student View** and check whether the scores work the way they should.

7. If it all works correctly, give yourself a pat on the back for having made a start in one of Moodle's more advanced activities! Your next step might be to try linking correct and incorrect responses to different pages, allowing you and your students to branch out even further!

Getting feedback from our students

It is important for our own professional development that we constantly strive to improve our teaching, and adapt it according to our successes and setbacks. For this, we need the input of our students (it's the Student Voice concept, for which Moodle is perfectly suited). We could use Moodle's **Choice activity** module as a very basic survey. But the issue with this is that the pupils are able to respond to only single word, or short phrase suggestions that we give them. If we want a more detailed evaluation of our efforts in Moodle, the **Feedback** module fits the bill perfectly, as we can include choice-type option button answers and also give them free rein to comment in the textboxes. And don't think that just because the students haven't reached double figures, they aren't capable of giving insightful opinions!

Time for action – setting up a feedback activity at the end of our course

We're going to find out what our class thinks of our course, by setting up a survey using Moodle's Feedback module.

1. In the section where you want the feedback, click the **Add an activity** drop-down and then **Feedback**.

     If you don't see **Feedback**, ask your Moodle admin to "open its eye" in the admin settings.

2. In **Name**, put a meaningful title the children will click on to get to the survey.

3. In **Description**, explain that this is for them to give their opinions on the course. Check the **Display description on course page** box if you want this to appear on your course home page.

4. Set the open and close times if you want.

5. Leave most of the **Feedback** options as they are but, choose whether you want students' names to be shown to you or not in **Record user names**. (They will never see each others' feedback)

6. In the **After submitting** box, type a *thank you for filling in this survey* type message.

7. Ignore the other settings and click on **Save and display**.

8. On the next screen, click the **Edit questions** tab.

9. On the screen that appears next, choose **Multiple choice**.

10. Add a question in the **Question** box, as I have done in the following screenshot, and click on **Save question**. (Leave any settings you don't understand.)

11. Now choose **Longer text answer** in the **Add question to activity** box.

12. Add a question as I have in the following screenshot. (Leave any settings you don't understand.)

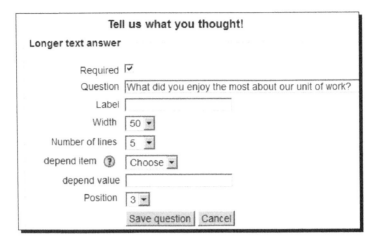

13. Add a couple more longer text questions yourself here. Perhaps they could be about what they did not like so much and how they think it could be made better?

14. Do you notice how each time we make a question, we can see it previewed as the students would view it?

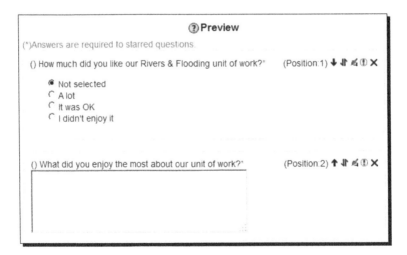

What just happened?

We set up a survey, a Moodle Feedback activity to gauge our students' appreciation of our Rivers and Flooding course.

But wait; we surely don't want them to complete this before they have done all the other activities? Sure we can set a date for it to open, but that still doesn't force them to do the other games and exercises first. We can hide the **Feedback** link ourselves with the eye icon, but we then need to manually unhide it when we need to open it up again.

Is there a way we can set our Feedback to open automatically once the children have done other activities? Can we schedule tasks and games so they only appear once the children have done the earlier ones? Yes! And we're going to take a look at how to do that right now!

Controlling the learning path with Conditional Activities

Conditional Activities is Moodle's fancy name for locking items down and only showing them to pupils under certain conditions. If your Moodle admin has enabled **Conditional access** along with **Completion tracking**, then at the end of each resource and activity we've set up, you will have noticed some settings like this:

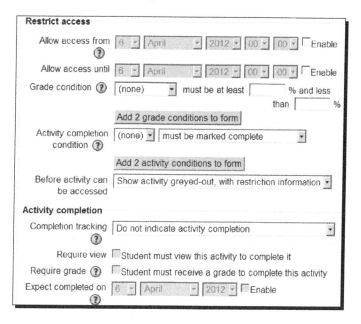

If your admin tells you everything is enabled sitewide, but you still don't see the settings, you can enable **Completion tracking** for your course in **Settings | Course administration | Edit settings**.

Until now, I've just said to ignore these settings. Now, however, we are going to use them to control what our children see and when.

We're going to follow our colleague, Stuart Gorse, who is teaching his nine year olds the French names of animals. He has a video he wants them to watch. After watching the video, they have to do an online text assignment and after the assignment, as a treat, they can play a SCORM **Fling the Teacher** game. But they only get to play the game once they've had their assignment graded by Mr Gorse! And they can only do the assignment once they have watched the video! In fact, when they first go to his course, they only see the video and don't even know the assignment or game exist!

Here's how to do it:

Time for action – scheduling conditional activities (1)

We are going to control the learning path of our students by setting conditions on the tasks they have to do. First, let's deal with the video:

1. Set up the video in a Page, the online text assignment, and the SCORM **Fling the Teacher** game.

2. Click on **Edit settings** for the Page with the video and scroll down to **Activity completion**.

3. Change the settings so that they are the same as mine in the next screenshot:

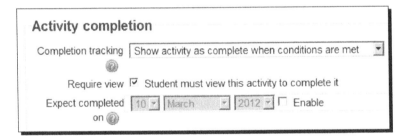

What just happened?

We have set a condition on Stuart's video page; the students can see the link to the page but for it to be marked as *complete* they have to watch the video. Or at least they have to click the link to get to the video page! Unless we are standing over them, we won't know if they have truly paid attention or not. But that's what the assignment is for.

So let's move on.

Time for action – scheduling conditional activities (2)

We're now going to set access conditions on the assignment:

1. Click on **Edit settings** for the assignment and scroll down to **Restrict access**.

2. In the **Activity Completion condition** box, choose the video page.

3. In the **Before activity can be accessed** box, choose **Hide activity entirely**.

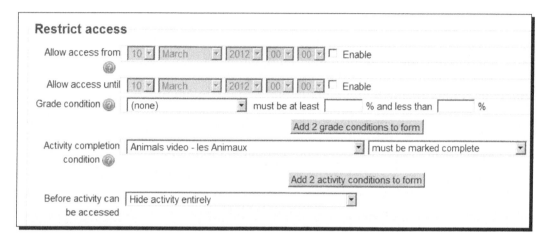

What just happened?

We set a condition upon the assignment such that it will only become visible once the student has completed the video page activity. And we already set the completion condition on the video page, in that they have to click on the page and (hopefully!) watch it. Once they have done that, the assignment will become visible.

But there's more....

Time for action – scheduling conditional activities (3)

As well as setting access conditions on the assignment, we also need to define how it will be marked as *complete*. Let's do that now:

1. Scroll down to **Activity Completion**.

2. Change the **Completion tracking** settings so they are the same as mine in the next screenshot:

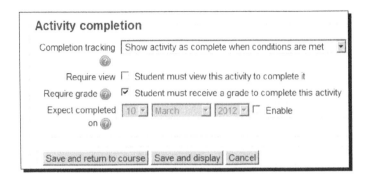

What just happened?

We set a completion condition upon the assignment; Stuart has to give them a grade before it will be marked as complete. Why does this matter? Because they won't be able to see or play the game until he does!

Let's move onto the final stage of our schedule.

Time for action – finalizing conditional activities

Let's now repeat the access and completion conditions for the game we want them to play:

1. Click on **Edit settings** for the game and scroll down to **Restrict access**.

2. In the **Activity Completion condition** box, choose the online text assignment.

3. In the **Before activity can be accessed** box, choose **Hide activity entirely**.

4. In the **Completion tracking** box, choose **Students can manually mark the activity as completed**.

What just happened?

We set a condition upon the SCORM game; the students can't see it until Stuart has given them a grade. Although we didn't have to, we set a completion condition upon the game too, which means they can themselves mark it as complete. If we take a look at the course page now from the teacher's point of view, we can get a better idea of how this feature works:

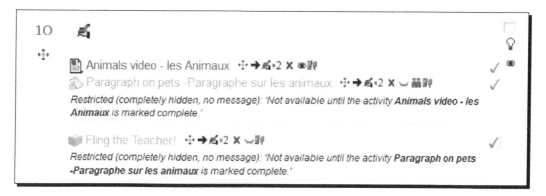

Stuart and other teachers can see the message telling them the tasks are hidden (as we'll see in a moment); the children see nothing! Note the checkmarks to the right as well. For the first two activities those checkmarks will automatically change color once the task is complete. For the last one, remember we set it to **Students can manually mark the activity as completed**? The children will be able to click the checkmark themselves when they have played the game.

Beware though that if you allow students to mark their work as complete themselves, there is nothing stopping them clicking the checkmark without even looking at the tasks!

Finally, let's see it from the children's point of view:

Not giving anything away! The children are forced to click on the video link if they want to see anything else on the course page!

Have a go hero – set this up in your course?

Now that we've seen how Stuart Gorse did this in his French course, why not go back to the Rivers and Flooding course and try out some conditional activities there? It might be a good idea to start with the **Feedback,** we set up a few pages back.

 Did you notice in **Restrict access** that there were other options we didn't use? You can set grades as conditions for example, and you can place a teasing, grayed out message to the student telling them there is a game there but they can't get to it until they have done the hard work of the assignment! (Personally I prefer to hide the activities completely; I think it is kinder.) Different activities offer different completion conditions too. If you are using a Forum, you can force them to post a message or reply to a message before they can move on. If you are using a Choice activity, you can force them to make a choice before they can access their next task.

Finishing off—what else can Moodle do for me?

In learning how to create a DME with a Lesson, and in setting access conditions on our activities, we looked at two slightly more advanced features of Moodle. There are many more features that Moodle has to offer to enhance our teaching, but not all of them are available on the standard Moodle website that most schools have installed. However, if you have a sympathetic Moodle administrator who has complete control of your Moodle installation, it is very easy to plugin extra options that can be very useful and also a lot of fun. One Moodler has compared Moodle to a Lego set. You start with the basic building bricks and then, as you become more experienced, you can add different types of bricks to fulfill different functions.

The next section will outline what you can do with some of the extra plugins available on the main Moodle site, `http://www.moodle.org`. The following table suggests a handful of plugins that I've found work well with children in the age group of 7-14. You might like to ask your administrator sweetly (or maybe bribe them with chocolate!) if they could add one or two of these to your school's Moodle course page. If your Moodle is brand new in June 2012 (ask your admin if it's *version 2.3*) you may well have the last one on the list anyway!

Optional plugin name	What it is	How we could use it
Certificate	Generates a personalized certificate.	Great for the end of our course!
Lightbox gallery	An easy image gallery that displays folders of photos in a flashy kind of way.	Useful for people such as our colleague Liz who want a simple way to display photos.
Game module	Takes words from the Glossary or Quiz and puts them into eight different types of games.	We can't have too many games that work with Moodle's gradebook.
Stamp collection	Gives students reward stamps.	A great motivator, just like gold stars in the students' books.
Book	Linked pages, a bit like a mini website	This will be standard in the new version of Moodle after June 2012 and is handy for showcasing students' work or setting out resources in a neat way.

Making our course home page look more like a web page

As we approach the end of the book, let's just take a look back at *Chapter 1, Getting Started*. There, I pointed out that for the young students we are teaching, appearance is everything. It was important for us to make our course page appealing to the eye, and so we spent some time in adding images, changing font styles and colors, and trying to keep our resources in a neat order. We have a busy course, full of content, now. Although our Moodle course has got lots to keep our youngsters occupied, it still has that rather conventional Moodle layout of different topic sections, where we have to scroll down to reach the activity that we want.

On ordinary websites, the pages are much shorter, and you can get to the other sections by clicking on the text or on image hyperlinks. Moodle offers some additional **course formats** (extra to the topics section format we've been using) and they help a great deal to make your course page easier to navigate. If you have a brand new version of Moodle after June 2012, your version of Moodle might have a page-like course format already, and your administrator can get other course formats from the same place they get those extra modules such as the certificate, so it's well worth asking.

But what if you're not able to do that at your school? What can we do with the standard topics format of Moodle to make it look like a normal web page instead of a Moodle course page? Let's be radical; let's redo the whole thing! Instead of having four sections with activities that stretch far down the page, let's just keep the page short, with an image for each unit. We could then click on the relevant image to take us to that unit's activities. We can have something similar to what is shown in the following screenshot:

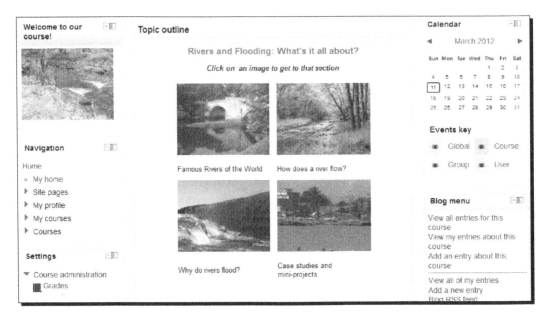

Our students can see everything in one window—no need to scroll down! But where are all the activities? And how is it done? We can't hide them using the *eye*, because then they are not accessible to students at all. Thus, we need to find some other cunning way of hiding them, but still making them available. But first, we need to set that top section up with the image links.

Have a go hero – source and resize suitable images for each topic section

The plan is to replace each numbered topic section with an image, which will hyperlink to the activities in that section. Your first mission, then, is to find some suitable images, such as `.jpg` photos or `.gif` clipart of your choice. Then, you have to make them all the same size, so that they look correct on the page. Mine are 160 X 120 pixels; that's not a bad size. 100 X 100 pixels might even be better if you want your image to be square in shape.

Got them? Now let's upload them into the course and let's get started!

Time for action – adding image links to our topic sections

Let's learn how to add images into our Moodle course, which when clicked, will take you to a new website.

1. With editing turned on, click on the editing icon for **Topic 0** in the toolbar, click on the **Insert Table** icon, located to the left-hand side of the letters **HTML** as in the next screenshot.

2. If you're copying my layout, choose two columns and four rows. Choose **0** for border, cell spacing, and padding.

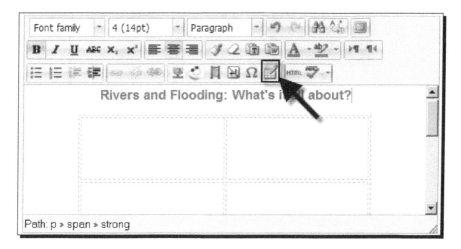

3. Click on the Full Screen Editor icon located at the top of the screen, on the far right-hand side.

4. Click in the upper-left cell.

5. Click on the image icon and upload your first topic image using the methods we're familiar with by now. Centre it by using centering icon in the text editor.

6. In the cell directly below the image icon, add the topic name and centre it.

7. Repeat this with the other three images and topic titles, as shown in the following screenshot:

8. Click the Full Screen Editor icon again to close it and save changes.

What just happened?

We went into the editing area of **Topic 0** and created a table, into which we added images that will link to our different units of work. We put the names of the units underneath, to help with identification. Eventually, this table in **Topic 0** will be all that the students will see and they will click on the images (or the text if you prefer) to access their work.

So now we need to create some pages to add our activities into. Then, we can link those pages to the relevant image in **Topic 0**. Let's start with **Topic 1—Famous Rivers of the World**.

Time for action – putting our activities into web pages

There are various ways to go about this, but the following way is the one that I prefer:

1. Open up a Word document, Notepad, or a similar text editing program into which you can paste some URLs.

2. Go to **Topic 1**, and right-click on the first resource or activity.

3. If you're using Internet Explorer, right-click and select **Copy shortcut**. If you're using Firefox, click on **Copy link location** and if you are using Google Chrome, click on **Copy link address**.

4. Copy (*Ctrl+C*) the address or the URL that will appear, and then paste it (*Ctrl+V*) into your text document.

5. In your text document, type a name to remind you which resource or activity the link was for.

6. Repeat this process with all of the resources and activities in **Topic 1**.

7. Keep your text document safe and scroll down to the bottom of the final topic.

8. Under **Add a resource**, choose **Page**.

9. Type in an introduction to the topic and paste in the resources and activities hyperlinks from your text document, making sure that they open in a new window.

10. Save and display it. It will look something like this:

In this topic we're going to investigate some famous rivers of the world. You'll learn about the longest, deepest, widest rivers throughout the globe ☺

Here is some information about rivers in the UK. If you can't get them to come up on your computer, you can download a program that will help you by clicking here

1. Click here to read about the Thames
2. Click here to read about the Severn
3. Click here for an information sheet about Rivers in Wales
4. Click here for an information sheet about Rivers in Scotland

Next up we're going around the World in Rivers...

Remember that because this is a page, we have the freedom to make it attractive, with images, hyperlinks, and so on. **Topic 1** looks pretty basic as it's just an introduction, with some word-processed documents. Just imagine how much fun we can have setting up the web page for our interactive, multimedia, Web 2.0 case studies in **Topic 4**!

What just happened?

Basically, we went to **Topic 1**, copied the links to the resources and activities by right-clicking and copying their URLs or web addresses, and then pasted them into a Moodle page, which we embellished with some friendly words and colorful images. The idea is that our students will click on the **Topic 1** image in **Topic 0** and this will take them directly to the **Topic 1** page. They can then select, from this page, the activity that they need to do next.

So we need to go back to that table of images in **Topic 0** and then link the page that we just developed to the first image. But that's easy for an advanced Moodler.

Time for action – link the topic page to its image

Just use the same principles as before. There's nothing new to learn here.

1. Right-click on the page and copy its URL.

2. Click the editing icon for **Topic 0** and click on the first image, which is for **Topic 1**.

3. Click on the hyperlink icon and paste the URL of the page into the hyperlink box.

4. Save, and check whether it works!

The same process, we went through for **Topic 1**, now needs to be repeated for the other three topics. Are you up for it?

Have a go hero – link the other topics to their images

It's just a question of taking a topic section, copying its resource links onto a new Moodle page, prettying up the web page, and then linking it to its matching image up at the top of our course. Once you have done that with all of the other sections, there is only one more job left to do, which is, to get the effect that we saw earlier.

Concealing our activities to make our course page neater

This is the crafty part! The secret is in hiding the topics within the activities—without closing their eyes or making the content unavailable.

Time for action – making our course page look more like a web page

Let's learn how to make our Moodle course page look prettier, and more like a web page.

1. In the **Settings** block, under the **Course administration** heading, click on **Edit settings**.

2. Change the number of topics to **0**.

3. Save your changes.

Done! Forget the coffee! Crack open the champagne!

What just happened?

We performed a massive con trick! We linked all our resources in sections 1 to 4 into **Topic 0**. We then got Moodle to display only **Topic 0** and keep the others out of sight. But just because we set the course to display only one topic, it doesn't mean that the others are gone forever. Our efforts over nine chapters can't be deleted that easily. They're just hiding, and waiting to be made available for use, but actually not on the page. Do you see that if you have your editing turned on, you see the words **Orphaned activities**? This is to remind you that the activities under that heading are not visible to the students, but easily there for you to change if you ever need to. Our students never see those words. They just see our images in **Topic 0**.

Summary

In this chapter, we've risen to the challenge of advanced Moodling, using our recently-acquired skills to tackle more complex features. We have created a Decision Making Exercise (DME) using a Moodle Lesson, got our students to evaluate our efforts with the Feedback activity, learned how to control what they do and when they do it with Conditional Activities, and gained an insight into some optional extras of Moodle, such as a Certificate. Finally we added a finishing touch to our course by making it look more like a web page.

We've learned that Moodle offers a wide variety of ways for our students to learn—from us, from each other, and also on their own. We've learned that working on Moodle isn't just about uploading word-processed worksheets (which might not even be viewable to some of our youngsters). Rather, it's about providing opportunities to engage, to explore, and above all to enjoy the pleasures of acquiring and evaluating new knowledge in a modern, multimedia environment.

I hope that you have as much fun using Moodle with your classes as I do. If you need any more help, come along to the forums on `http://www.moodle.org`, where there are over a million enthusiasts, myself included, who will be keen to provide you with assistance.

Happy Moodling!

Index

Fling the Teacher game
  about 132
  creating 134-136
  playing 138
  setting up 132, 133
  uploading, on Moodle 136-138
Flip-Flap game 127

G

glossary 59
Google Maps
  displaying, on Moodle 169, 170
  warning 171

H

handlebar 196
Hot potatoes
  about 82
  differentiated exercises, creating 92
  downloading 82
  drag-and-drop activity, for rivers and continents
      88, 89
  installing 82
  JMatch, used for matching rivers with conti-
      nents 84, 85
  matching activity, uploading to Moodle 89
  multimedia, adding 100
  registering 83
  scores, saving in Moodle 100
  self-marking activities, creating 82
  self-marking crossword exercise, creating witjh
      JCross 93-95
  self-marking gap-fill exercise, creating with
      JCloze 90-92
  self-marking mixed up words exercise, creating
      with JMix 96, 97
  self-marking multiple-choice quiz, creating with
      JQuiz 98, 99
  URL 82
  warning 100
Hot Potatoes activities scores
  saving, in Moodle 100
Hot Potatoes exercises
  JCloze 84
  JCross 84
  JMatch 84

  JMix 84
  JQuiz 84
  The Masher 84
HTML 17
HTML block
  about 15, 17
  configuring 16, 17
  images, adding 25, 26

I

i-devices
  Moodle, using 204
image links
  adding, to topic sections 227, 228
images
  adding, to HTML block 25, 26
  Flickr, using for uploading 24
  resizing 199-201
  resizing, IrfanView used 198, 199
  uploading, to course page 20-23
iMovie 153
interactive Flash files
  uploading, to Moodle 194, 195
Internet Explorer (IE) 40
iPads
  advantages 204
  disadvantages 205
IrfanView
  about 197
  download link 197
  installing 197, 198
  URL 197
  used, for resizing photo in Moodle 198, 199
iSpring Free
  about 194
  URL 193

J

JCloze potato
  used, for creating differentiated exercises 92
  used, for creating self-marking gap-fill exercise
      90-92
JCross potato
  used, for creating self-marking crossword
      exercise 93-95

Thank you for buying
Moodle 2 for Teaching 7-14 Year Olds

About Packt Publishing

Packt, pronounced 'packed', published its first book "*Mastering phpMyAdmin for Effective MySQL Management*" in April 2004 and subsequently continued to specialize in publishing highly focused books on specific technologies and solutions.

Our books and publications share the experiences of your fellow IT professionals in adapting and customizing today's systems, applications, and frameworks. Our solution based books give you the knowledge and power to customize the software and technologies you're using to get the job done. Packt books are more specific and less general than the IT books you have seen in the past. Our unique business model allows us to bring you more focused information, giving you more of what you need to know, and less of what you don't.

Packt is a modern, yet unique publishing company, which focuses on producing quality, cutting-edge books for communities of developers, administrators, and newbies alike. For more information, please visit our website: www.packtpub.com.

About Packt Open Source

In 2010, Packt launched two new brands, Packt Open Source and Packt Enterprise, in order to continue its focus on specialization. This book is part of the Packt Open Source brand, home to books published on software built around Open Source licences, and offering information to anybody from advanced developers to budding web designers. The Open Source brand also runs Packt's Open Source Royalty Scheme, by which Packt gives a royalty to each Open Source project about whose software a book is sold.

Writing for Packt

We welcome all inquiries from people who are interested in authoring. Book proposals should be sent to author@packtpub.com. If your book idea is still at an early stage and you would like to discuss it first before writing a formal book proposal, contact us; one of our commissioning editors will get in touch with you.

We're not just looking for published authors; if you have strong technical skills but no writing experience, our experienced editors can help you develop a writing career, or simply get some additional reward for your expertise.

Moodle 2.0 E-Learning Course Development

ISBN: 978-1-84951-526-9   Paperback: 344 pages

A complete guide to successful learning using Moodle

1. The new book and ebook edition of the best selling introduction to using Moodle for teaching and e-learning, updated for Moodle 2.0

2. Straightforward coverage of installing and using the Moodle system, suitable for newcomers as well as existing Moodle users who want to get a few tips

3. A unique course-based approach focuses your attention on designing well-structured, interactive, and successful courses

Moodle 2 for Teaching 4-9 Year Olds Beginner's Guide

ISBN: 978-1-84951-328-9   Paperback: 332 pages

Use Moodle to create quizzes, puzzles, and games to enhance the learning ability of your students

1. A beginner's guide with lots of practical examples

2. Learn how to create a wealth of exciting activities to make teaching and learning fun

3. Minimize the stress of lesson planning with lots of exercises that can be used again and again

4. Written to Moodle 2, the examples in this book can also be used in previous versions of Moodle

Please check **www.PacktPub.com** for information on our titles